ASSESSING MATH CONCEPTS

Kathy Richardson

Assessment Eight

GROUPING TENS

Design, Layout and Editorial Advisor: Janann Roodzant
Layout Assistant: JoEllen Key
Editor: Karen Antell
Illustrations: Linda Starr
Front Cover Design: Lori Young, *Lori I Young Design*
Cover Design/Coordinator: Kenneth W. Harris II, *Mad Monkey Media*

This book is published by Mathematical Perspectives

Mathematical Perspectives Teacher Development Center
P.O. Box 29418
Bellingham, WA 98228-9418
Phone: 360-715-2782

This book is printed on recycled paper.

Distributed by Didax, Inc.

Didax
395 Main Street
Rowley, MA 01969-1207
800-458-0024
www.didaxinc.com

ISBN 0-9724238-2-6

DEDICATION

This series of assessments is dedicated to my sister, Janann Roodzant, with more love, gratitude, and respect than I can ever say. And to our parents, Jim and Alice Young, who taught us that in the end, love is all that really matters.

PROFESSIONAL DEVELOPMENT SUPPORT

For information on the Mathematical Perspectives Professional Development Training to support teachers using the *Assessing Math Concepts* assessment series, contact:

Mathematical Perspectives Teacher Development Center
P.O. Box 29418
Bellingham, WA 98228-9419
Phone: 360-715-2782 Fax: 360-715-2783
www.mathperspectives.com

STUDENT INTERVIEW FORMS

To purchase the Assessing Math Concepts Student Interview forms, contact:

Didax, Inc., Distributor
395 Main Street
Rowley, MA 01969-1207
Phone: 1-800-433-4329
www.didaxinc.com

CREDITS

Richardson, Kathy. (1999). *Developing Number Concepts Series: Book 1 Counting, Comparing and Pattern; Book 2 Addition and Subtraction; Book 3 Place Values; Multiplication and Division; Planning Guide.* Parsippany, New Jersey: Pearson Education, Inc., publishing as Dale Seymour Publications.®

TABLE OF CONTENTS

Acknowledgments vi
The Assessment Series vii
Preface ix

INTRODUCTION TO THE ASSESSMENT SERIES 1
   How the Guides to the Assessments Are Organized 1
   The Mathematics: What Do Children Need to Learn? 3
      What is Basic? Learning Procedures or the Underlying Mathematics? 3
      The Development of Number Concepts 6
      Critical Learning Phases: The Key to Effective Instruction 7
   The Assessments: How Do We Know They're Learning? 11
      Overview of the Assessments 11
      Assessment Guidelines 15
      Using the Assessments for Classroom Instruction 17
      Using the Assessments for Interventions 21

GROUPING TENS ASSESSMENT 25
   Learning About Numbers as Tens and Ones 26
   The Challenges of Learning to Think of Numbers as Tens and Ones 27
   The Assessment Tools 28
   The Student Interview 29
      Examples of the Student Interview 31
      Student Interview Form, Page One 34
      Understanding the Recording Form and Indicators (for Page One) 35
      Student Interview Form, Page Two 43
      Understanding the Recording Form and Indicators (for Page Two) 44
   Meeting Instructional Needs 49
      The Class Summary Sheets 49
   Assessing Children at Work 54
      Assessing at Work Form, "Measuring Shapes" 55
   Linking Assessment and Instruction 57

APPENDIX: BLACKLINE MASTERS 63

ACKNOWLEDGMENTS

My search to understand how children learn mathematics became a passion for me during my first year of teaching 38 years ago. I remember so well how helpless I felt as a teacher as I looked down at 6-year-old Joey's workbook page to see that he had written a "1" as the answer for every problem on the page. "Joey, what are you doing?" I asked. I will never forget the look on Joey's face when he looked up at me and asked, "Why you always mad to me?" I realized then that I wasn't "mad to" Joey. I could see that he wasn't trying to avoid doing his work. In fact, he was trying to finish an assignment that made no sense to him in the only way he knew how. My frustration was not with him but with my own lack of knowledge. I didn't know why the workbook page that looked so easy to me was so hard for him. I didn't know what to do to help him make sense of it. Thus began my journey to understand how children learn mathematics and my search for ways to help children make sense of the mathematics they are asked to do. My passion for this work has never left me and my search has taken me to many schools throughout the county and allowed me to work with hundreds of children and teachers.

To all those teachers and children who have helped me along the way: thank you for sharing this journey with me.

A special thanks to those teachers who have worked with me over time as I refined the assessments and worked to make the assessment forms more useful. There are too many of you to name but please find yourself in this list and know how grateful I am to you.

Clark County School District , Las Vegas, NV
  MASE Project Teacher Leaders
  MAPS (Math Assessment for Primary Students) Selected Schools involved in the field test of the assessment forms
  Sue Plummer and Lori Squires: Project Leaders

Visalia Unified School District, Visalia, CA
  STEPPS: Math coaches, teacher leaders and classroom teachers

Larabee School, Bellingham, WA
  Cathy Young, math coach

Childs Elementary School, Bloomington, IN
  Chris Oster, teacher

Edmonds School District, Edmonds, Washington
  Edmonds Math Project: Teacher Leaders

There are some people I can never thank enough for all that they have done to help me get this project completed. A special thanks to Janann Roodzant who is the most giving person I know, to Sheryl Russell who is endlessly patient with my struggles to get things right, and to my husband, Tom, for his undying support and encouragement.

And to another very special group of people that make my work possible: A thank you from the bottom of my heart to my friends and colleagues at Mathematical Perspectives: Teacher Development Center. I am grateful every day that you have chosen to be a part of my work and my life.

THE ASSESSMENT SERIES

Assessing Math Concepts

Assessment 1: COUNTING OBJECTS

Assessment 2: CHANGING NUMBERS

Assessment 3: MORE/LESS TRAINS

Assessment 4: NUMBER ARRANGEMENTS

Assessment 5: COMBINATION TRAINS

Assessment 6: THE HIDING ASSESSMENT

Assessment 7: TEN FRAMES

Assessment 8: GROUPING TENS

Assessment 9: TWO-DIGIT ADDITION AND SUBTRACTION

PREFACE

Observing children as they face the challenges of growing and learning is an endlessly fascinating, sometimes puzzling, and always intriguing undertaking. I remember the day many years ago when I decided to accompany my colleague, Margie Gonzales, to the playground for yard duty. While we were discussing some aspect of our ongoing quest to understand how children learn, Anthony, one of her second grade students who had been struggling to learn to read, came running over to her. "Mrs. Gon-gol-es, I know my sight words!" he said with great excitement and pride. Then he proceeded to recite the list of words he had been asked to study, but without benefit of any piece of paper on which the words were written. "Is, of, from, to, on, with…," he said, showing, in spite of his reading difficulty, an ability to learn whatever he believed the school had set out for him–whether it made sense or not. This was a major accomplishment for Anthony. He had worked very hard to memorize that list of words. His time and energy had been spent on something that looked like reading to him but that served him not at all as a reader. This experience with Anthony, who had worked so hard to learn the wrong thing, has come to represent for me all children diligently trying to learn whatever they believe is expected–even when it makes no sense–even when it is the wrong thing.

Anthony came to mind many times in my early years as a teacher, especially when I was teaching mathematics. I observed children working hard to learn the mathematics in front of them. Most of them learned to do the tasks and were able to get right answers, but they seemed to be learning the wrong things. Children who had learned to say the sequence for counting by fives counted objects by moving one at a time instead of five at a time. Children who were able to label the tens and ones in a number counted on their fingers when asked to add 10 to a number. Children who could recite "4 plus 4 is 8" were unable to use that information to solve 4 + 5. Children would carefully follow steps to get answers but were unable to tell if their answers made sense or not. These children, like Anthony, were learning to do what was expected, but what they were learning was not what they needed to know. They could get right answers but did not understand the underlying mathematics with which they were working.

This lack of understanding, so evident in the children with whom I was working, left me with the following questions:

"What are the foundational mathematical ideas children need to know?" and
"How do we know they're learning these important ideas?"

This series of assessments is the result of my search to understand what children need to know to be successful in their study of mathematics and my desire to provide teachers with the tools they need to provide effective and appropriate experiences for their students.

INTRODUCTION TO THE
ASSESSMENT SERIES

Assessing Math Concepts is a continuum of assessments that focuses on important core concepts and related "Critical Learning Phases" that must be in place if children are to understand and be successful in mathematics. This assessment series is based on the premise that teachers will be able to provide more effective instruction and ensure maximum learning for each of their students when they are aware of the essential steps that children move through when developing an understanding of foundational mathematical ideas. The data that is gathered and organized using the assessment tools presented here provides teachers with the information that is needed to determine precisely what children need to learn. Students progress confidently when teachers are able to provide appropriately challenging learning experiences for individuals and classroom groups.

The Grouping Tens Assessment is eighth in a series of nine books that form the assessment component focusing on numbers to 100. This guide gives the teacher the needed background information for giving and using the assessment tasks, organizing the information, and doing classroom observations. Guidelines for providing appropriate instruction and references to selected resources are included. Copies of these copyrighted Student Interview forms (S.I. forms) are available from the publisher as they are not to be reproduced. Blackline masters of the Classroom Summary sheets (C.S. sheets) used for collecting data and the Assessing at Work forms (A.W. forms) for documenting observations of specific skills while the children are at work in the classroom are included and may be reproduced for classroom use.

How the Guides to the Assessments Are Organized

Introduction
The guide for each assessment includes an introduction to the assessment series as a whole. The introduction discusses the mathematics that children need to learn and presents an overview of all of the assessments in the series. Information is also provided that helps teachers choose the appropriate assessments for planning classroom instruction and for identifying children who may need some kind of intervention.

The Assessment
Each guide includes the following sections that describe the assessment and how to use it.

I: Learning about the Concept
This section provides the background information that teachers need in order to understand how children develop the concept being assessed. Learning goals related to the concept are listed along with the critical learning phases that children must reach if they are to achieve the goals.

II: The Student Interview

An overview of the structure of the Student Interview is presented next to help teachers become familiar with the procedure they are to follow and the questions they are to ask the students. This is followed by examples of actual interviews. The examples help teachers see how the interview unfolds and what kinds of responses they can expect children to make.

Examples of the Student Interview forms and explanations of each section of the interview follow. The actual interview takes just a few minutes to administer. However, there is a great deal of information that can be obtained when teachers know what to look for and how to interpret what they see. Therefore, detailed information about the intent of each of the questions and an explanation of each of the indicators is included.

III: Meeting Instructional Needs

This section presents examples of the Class Summary sheets. These sheets provide a place to organize data so teachers can identify children with similar needs. Also included are guidelines for planning appropriate experiences to meet a range of needs.

IV: Assessing Children at Work

Once the individual interview is given, teachers will be able to observe children's progress over time while they are at work. To assist in this process, an assessment task designed for small groups of students is presented in this section. An example of the Assessing at Work form is included, along with an explanation of the assessment task.

V: Linking Assessment and Instruction

This section describes the instructional needs for each of the indicators on the assessment and refers teachers to the particular activities from the *Developing Number Concept* series to aid those who have access to these resources. Links to other curricula can also be made using the results of these assessment materials.

Appendix of Blackline Masters

Included in this section are blackline masters that individual teachers may reproduce for their own classroom use. They include the Class Summary sheet(s), the Assessing at Work forms, and, when necessary, the masters needed for the Assessing at Work task.

THE MATHEMATICS:
What Do Children Need to Learn?

Mathematics is a complex and multi-faceted discipline that has importance in many areas of human endeavor. It helps us understand the world we live in, from the natural environment to the latest technologies. We use it daily to analyze situations and to solve problems. If the study of mathematics is to be valuable for students, they must learn that mathematics is an important and powerful tool that helps them explore and make sense of the world.

Children's earliest experiences with mathematics build the foundation for the work they will be asked to do in coming years. If children are to be successful in the study of mathematics throughout their schooling, it is vital that the mathematics they learn be meaningful to them. It is only then that they can build on these early experiences.

Far too many children are never given the opportunity to learn that mathematics is a sense-making process. For them, the study of mathematics requires memorizing rules and procedures in order to complete tasks and to get right answers. What they learn turns out to be a set of dead-end skills rather than necessary foundational understandings. In many situations, they are expected to do whatever mathematics has been assigned to their particular grade level whether or not they have the background knowledge they need to understand the mathematics they are asked to do. If they have trouble completing assignments, they are shown how to do the tasks again, and if necessary, they are walked through the required steps. What is missing in this approach is the identification of the foundational ideas necessary for understanding the mathematics inherent in the work the children are expected to do. Rather than repeating a process the child does not understand, it is important to determine what mathematics the child knows and what the child still needs to learn.

What is Basic?
Learning Procedures or the Underlying Mathematics?

There are many children who are successful in completing math assignments but who are not learning the essential mathematics necessary for future success in their study of mathematics. If teachers are to know what they need to do to ensure that children are learning the important foundational ideas, they must understand what mathematics the children are (or are not) learning when completing certain kinds of tasks. They must recognize that what is required of children when they are asked to solve problems using procedures (whether they understand them or not) is different from what is required of children who are asked to demonstrate an understanding of the underlying mathematics.

The following example points out what children need to know in order to get an answer using memorized procedures. This is followed by a description of what children will know if they have learned the mathematics inherent in the problem.

The Problem: 48 + 57

Method One: Getting Answers by Using Procedures
Consider what the children know when they solve the problem using procedures rather than using mathematics.

Step 1 First you have to line up the digits in the correct places:

```
 48
+57
```

Step 2 The digits on the right are labeled "ones." The digits on the left are labeled "tens."

You start with the ones first: 8 + 7 is 15.
(This answer may be arrived at because it has been memorized or more often because children count up from 8 saying 8, 9, 10, 11, 12, 13, 14, 15.)

Step 3 You put down the 5 and carry the 1.

```
 1
 48
+57
   5
```

Step 4 Then you add the tens. 1 plus 4 is 5 and 5 more is 10.

```
 1
 48
+57
105
```

The answer is 105.

When children learn to add, subtract, multiply and divide as a set of procedures and do not also see the underlying logic of the mathematics with which they are working, they may be able to get correct answers, but what they have learned is limited and useful only for solving those particular types of problems. They approach each problem in the same way and do not make connections between one type of problem and another or use what they know to solve similar problems. When children are focused on the procedures rather than the number relationships, they are often unable to tell if their answers are reasonable or not. If they happen to forget a step (such as carrying the 1) they can easily end up with the answer of 915, usually with no concern for whether or not the answer makes numerical sense.

When children learn only to follow procedures without understanding the underlying mathematics, what they are doing is empty of mathematics. Therefore, it is simply not possible for them to build on what has been learned when and if they are asked to deal with more complex ideas. This way of learning mathematics not only limits the ability of students to see relationships and to make connections, but more profoundly, it leads to an attitude towards all mathematics learning which can be summed up by a common comment, "I don't want to know why. Just show me what to do."

On the other hand, when children learn computation as part of the study of important mathematical ideas related to number, they are not only competent when dealing with computational problems, but they also will have learned more mathematics, as we see in the following example.

Method Two: Understanding the Underlying Mathematics
Consider what children know when they have learned the underlying mathematics inherent in the problem   48 + 57=

A child who knows the underlying structure of the numbers and their relationships to other numbers might make the following kinds of observations as he or she solves the problem:

> "The answer must be close to 100 because 48 is almost 50 and 57 is a little more than 50.
> Numbers are composed of tens and ones; the 4 is worth 40 and the 5 is worth 50.
> 4 tens and 5 tens make 9 tens. 9 tens is worth 90.
> Since 8 and 2 more makes ten, I can take 2 from the 7 to make a ten.
> 7 less 2 leaves 5. 10 and 5 is 15.
> 90 and 15 make 100 and 5 more. 100 and 5 more is 105."

Or another child might consider the following relationships:

> "48 is 2 less than 50.
> I can take 2 from the 57 to make the 48 into 50.
> 50 and 50 is 100.
> 7 minus the 2 (to make 50) is 5.
> 48 + 57 is 100 and 5 more. That totals 105."

It may take less time in the short run for children to learn the procedures for getting answers than it takes to learn the underlying mathematical concepts. However, simply getting answers is not enough. Learning the essential mathematics is what matters. If the focus is primarily on helping children memorize procedures in order to arrive at answers, children are robbed of important mathematical learning. However, if children are given opportunities to focus on the underlying mathematics, their study of computation can be a critical part of their study of mathematics and can help them develop mathematical thinking and reasoning. They will learn not only how to add, subtract, multiply and divide, but they will also learn number relationships, number composition and decomposition, and the underlying structure of the number system. When children study computation in ways that allow them to understand the inherent mathematics, they are able to work with numbers with understanding and efficiency and are able to build on the mathematics they have learned when studying other areas of mathematics, including fractions, decimals, and percents. Since they are doing mathematics rather than following procedures that are meaningless to them, they are also being prepared for the study of more advanced topics such as algebra and discrete mathematics. Because children's early mathematical experiences have such a profound effect on their future success, teachers must be clear about what mathematics the children should learn in these first years of school and must have ways to determine if the concepts and skills children are learning are meaningful to them.

The Development of Number Concepts

What children know and understand about number and number relationships impacts every other area of mathematical study. Children cannot analyze data, determine functional relationships, compare measures of area and volume or describe relative lengths of sides unless they can use numbers in meaningful ways. Number concepts are the foundation that children must have in order to achieve high standards in mathematics as a whole.

The important mathematics that children must learn to solve problems has been organized for this set of assessments into the following core topics:

Counting

Number Relationships

Number Composition and Decomposition to 20

Place Value: Number Composition and Decomposition of Numbers to 100

Counting
When children first learn to count, they think of numbers as one and another one and another one. I refer to this stage as the "Count and Land" stage. As children develop competence, they will not only count with accuracy and ease in a variety of situations, but they will also develop a sense of the quantity of the numbers they are working with. Their focus will move from knowing what number they landed on to making reasonable estimates and noting the reasonableness of the outcome of their counting.

Beginning Number Relationships
After children learn to count, their next task is to build a sense of quantities and relationships between those quantities. The first relationships children learn are usually "one more" and "one less." Later, children begin to think about the quantity itself in relationship to other quantities and begin to make comparisons between numbers.

Number Composition and Decomposition to 20
Before children are able to decompose numbers, they need to recognize that the smaller numbers are contained in the larger numbers and be able to describe the parts of numbers. That is, they will see that the quantity of 7 is not just a collection of ones, but is composed of 3 and 3 and 1 more. With experience composing and decomposing numbers, they will know the parts of numbers and see how they relate to other numbers so well that they will be able to add and subtract with automaticity. For example, they will know that 3 and 4 must be 7 because 3 and 3 are 6 and 1 more is 7. Or they will know that 3 and 4 are 7 so 7-3 must be 4. They will also know that 8 and 8 is 16, so 8 and 7 must be 15.

Place Value: Thinking of Numbers as Tens and Ones
Once children begin to work with larger numbers, they need to recognize the underlying structure of numbers as tens and ones. To do this, children must be able to count groups of tens as though they were single entities. They must also recognize that when you know the numbers of tens and ones you automatically know the total. When they understand that numbers are composed of tens and ones, they will be able to add 10 and subtract 10 without counting.

Place Value: Addition and Subtraction of Two-Digit Numbers
When children understand numbers as tens and ones and know the parts of numbers to 10, they will able to use what they know to combine numbers by forming all the tens possible and determining the number of leftovers. When subtracting, they can use what they know about numbers to break tens apart and recombine what is left.

Critical Learning Phases: The Key to Effective Instruction

As children develop an understanding of these core topics, there are certain essential ideas that are milestones, or hurdles in their growth of understanding. I have identified these stages of learning as Critical Learning Phases. According to the dictionary, a phase is "A particular moment or stage in a process, especially one at which a significant change or development occurs or a particular condition is reached." The Critical Learning Phase that a child has reached determines the way he or she is able to think with numbers and use numbers to solve problems.

For each major mathematical idea, there are certain understandings that must be in place to ensure that children are not just imitating procedures or saying words they don't really understand. When children receive instruction before they have the foundational ideas necessary to understand the mathematics present in the problems they are asked to solve, the best they can do is memorize the steps for getting right answers to these problems. This creates what I call an "illusion of learning" that breaks down at the point when true understanding becomes necessary for further growth. Children who do not see the underlying logic of the mathematics they are working with learn, over time, to stop looking for meaning and to focus only on procedures.

Sometimes the indicators that reveal whether a child understands or does not understand the mathematics he or she is working with are overlooked because the child appears to know in certain situations, and assumptions are made that the child knows more about the concept than he or she really does. For example, a child may have learned to line up cubes and carefully touch each one and tell how many. However, if the child is not able to hold a number in mind, they will count past that number when asked to get that number of objects. A child may be able to count a group of objects in a variety of settings, but if he is still thinking of each number as distinct from every other number, he may be unable to add to that group of objects to make another group and will build a whole new group instead. A child may have memorized the chant, "6 and 6 is 12", but it can be assumed she doesn't really know the meaning behind what she is saying unless she can use what she knows to solve 6 + 7. A child may be able to say that 3 tens and 4 is 34 but doesn't really understand the underlying structure of these numbers unless he can also tell how many there will be if 10 more were added.

Each of the assessments in the series identifies instructional goals for each concept and the related Critical Learning Phases that are important to the development of these core concepts. An overview of the Critical Learning Phases for Numbers to 100 are listed on the following pages.

THE CRITICAL LEARNING PHASES FOR NUMBERS TO 100

Phase: A particular moment or stage in a process, especially one at which a significant change or development occurs or a particular condition is reached.

The critical learning phase that a child has reached determines the way he or she is able to think with numbers and to use numbers to solve problems.

COUNTING

Counts Objects

- Gets a particular quantity
- Keeps track when counting objects
- Remembers how many after counting
- Counts objects by groups (2s, 5s, and 10s)

NUMBER RELATIONSHIPS

Knows One More/One Less

- Knows one more without counting
- Knows one less without counting

Is Developing a Sense of Quantity/Reasonableness

- Reacts to number estimated while counting
- Adjusts estimate while counting and makes a closer estimate

Relates One Number to Another Number

When changing one number to another:
- Tells whether they need to take some away or get some more
- Adds on or takes away by counting on or removing extras
- Knows (tells) how many to add or take away

Compares Numbers

When comparing two different groups:
- Uses what is known about one amount to determine another:
  Ex. This train has 8. This train has 2 more, so there must be 10.
- Adds or takes away from one group to make it the same as another group
- Tells how many more when groups are lined up
  - when the difference is 1 or 2
  - when the difference is more than 2
- Tells how many more when not lined up
- Tells how many less when the groups are lined up
  - when the difference is 1
  - when the difference is more than 1

NUMBER COMPOSITION AND DECOMPOSITION TO 20

Recognizes Parts of Numbers to 10 in Arrangements

- Recognizes groups of numbers to 5 in a variety of configurations
- Recognizes and describes the smaller parts contained in larger numbers
- Identifies one or more parts and counts the rest (counting on)
- Combines parts of arrangements by knowing

Knows Number Combinations

- Combines parts using relationships
- Knows doubles
- Uses doubles plus one
- Uses doubles minus one
- Combines parts by knowing

Decomposes Numbers to 10

- Figures out the missing part
- Knows the missing part without figuring out

Recognizes Numbers as One Ten and Some More

- Describes a ten as a single entity even though it is composed of 10 single objects
- Organizes numbers into groups of one ten and leftovers
- Knows 10 plus any number from 1 to 10
- Tells how many needed to make 10
- Tells how many leftovers when removing 10 for numbers from 11 to 20
- Combines quantities by reorganizing into one ten and leftovers
- Subtracts quantities by breaking numbers apart and recombining whatever is left

NUMBERS AS TENS AND ONES

Recognizes Numbers as Tens and Ones

- Forms and counts groups of tens
- Knows total instantly when number of tens and ones is known
- Knows 10 more for any two-digit number
- Knows 10 less for any two-digit number

Combines and Separates Tens and Ones

- Tells how many needed to make the next ten
- Combines numbers by forming new tens and leftovers when necessary
- Breaks apart tens when necessary and reorganizes what is left into tens and leftovers

THE ASSESSMENTS:
How Do We Know They're Learning?

This continuum of assessments follows the stages of children's development of the Critical Learning Phases for the core concepts for numbers to 100. The assessments pinpoint what children know and still need to learn and can be used to document children's growth over time.

Teachers can be misled into thinking that children are making the progress necessary to move on to more complex ideas when they get right answers without understanding the underlying mathematics. Therefore, these assessments are designed to yield more information than whether the children can "get it right or wrong." They determine not only their ability to get right answers but identify the actual mathematics the children know as well.

What young children know and understand can never be fully determined through paper and pencil tasks. Teachers can get much more complete and useful information if they watch and interact with the children while they are doing mathematical tasks. How the children respond indicates what Critical Learning Phase they have reached and reveals their level of understanding. Indicators that describe the range of responses and identify children's instructional needs are listed on each of the assessment forms and explained in detail in each book in the series.

Overview of the Assessments

The assessment described in this book is one of a set of nine. The following charts describe the concepts that are assessed in each book in the series and will help teachers see where the assessment they are using fits into the development of number concepts as a whole.

Topic	Assessments	Focus Questions	Range
Counting	**Concept 1:** *Counting Objects* Student Interview: "Counting Objects" Assessing at Work: "Counting Collections"	**Counting** • Can the children use counting confidently and accurately to find out how many? • Can they count out a particular amount? **One More/One Less** • Do they know one more and one less without counting?	**Task 1:** Counting an unorganized group of objects - from 1 or 2 objects to 32 objects **Task 2:** Counting out from 5 to 18 objects **Task 3:** Telling 1 more and 1 less within the range of numbers from 3 to 22 **Extension:** Telling 1 more and 1 less over the decades and beyond 100

Topic	Assessments	Focus Questions	Range
Number Relationships	**Concept 2:** *Beginning Number Relationships* Student Interview: "Changing Numbers" Assessing at Work: "Fix It"	• Can the children use the relationships between numbers to add or take away the appropriate group of objects to change one number into another? • Do they know particular relationships between numbers?	From adding 3 objects to 2 objects to form a group of 5, to knowing how many to add to 11 to make 15
	Concept 3: *Comparing Numbers* Student Interview: "More/Less Trains" Assessing at Work: "Comparing Yarn" and "Comparing Collections"	• Can the children use what they know about one quantity to determine another? • Can they tell how many more or less one number is than another?	From using one train to determine the length of the other, to determining how many more or less one quantity is than another Settings: Comparing two trains up to 11 cubes long with differences from 1 to 3; Comparing parts of a train (6, 4); Comparing two piles with differences of 3 (6 and 9, 9 and 12)

Topic	Assessments	Focus Questions	Range
Addition and Subtraction to 20	**Concept 4:** ***Identifying and Combining Parts*** Student Interview: "Number Arrangements" Assessing at Work: "Sorting Arrangement Cards"	• Can the children recognize small groups without counting? • Can they recognize and describe the parts of numbers in arrangements?	Instant recognition of the parts of numbers from 3 to 6 Recognizing and combining parts of numbers to 10
	Concept 5: ***Number Combinations*** Student Interview: "Combination Trains" Assessing at Work: "Number Combination Cards"	• Can they use what they know about one combination to figure out a related combination? • Can they combine parts to 10 without counting? • Can they combine parts to 20 without counting?	Combining related combinations from 2+1 to 8+8
	Concept 6: ***Decomposing Numbers to 10*** Student Interview: "Hiding Assessment" Assessing at Work: "Grab Bag Subtraction"	• Can they tell the missing part of a number (subtracting) without having to figure it out?	Identifying the missing parts of numbers from 3 to 10
	Concept 7: ***One Ten and Some More*** Student Interview: "Ten Frames" Part One: Combining Part Two: Taking Away Assessing at Work: "Can You Make a Ten?" "Can You Break Up a Ten?"	• Can they tell how many are needed to make the next ten? • Can they combine 2 single digit numbers to form a ten and leftovers? • Can they subtract a single digit number from a teen number by breaking up a ten?	**Addition:** From adding 10+8 to 8+7 **Extension:** 18+7 **Subtraction:** From subtracting 17-7 to 13-7 **Extension:** 23-7

Topic	Assessments	Focus Questions	Range
Place Value: Number Composition and Decomposition to 100	**Concept 8:** ***Numbers as Tens and Ones*** Student Interview: "Grouping Tens" Part One: Organizing into Tens Part Two: Conservation and Counting Groups Assessing at Work: "Measuring Shapes"	• Can they tell the total amount of a group of objects if they know the number of tens and ones? • Can they add ten more without counting? • Can they take ten away without counting?	**Task 1:** From determining how many in 3 groups of 10 and 4 ones by counting by ones, to knowing 10 more and 10 less without counting **Extension:** From determining 20 more and 20 less by counting, to knowing without counting Knowing what 7 tens and 12 ones total **Task 2:** From not understanding counting by 2s and 5s to counting by 2s and 5s with ease
	Concept 9: ***Combining and Separating Tens and Ones*** Student Interview: "Two-Digit Addition and Subtraction" Part One: Adding up Tens Part Two: Breaking up Tens Assessing at Work: "Tens and Ones Grid Shapes"	• Can they combine quantities by forming new tens when necessary? • Can they subtract from groups of tens and ones efficiently using relationships?	**Part One:** From solving two-digit addition problems by counting all, to solving problems by combining numbers into tens and ones using their knowledge of the parts of numbers **Part Two:** From solving two-digit subtraction problems by counting all, to solving problems by breaking numbers apart and recombining them using their knowledge of parts of numbers

Assessment Guidelines

There are two ways that information about the child's level of understanding and competence with concepts is gathered: 1) through student interviews and 2) through assessing children while they are at work.

The Student Interview
The student interviews help teachers become familiar with the stages through which children move as they develop particular concepts. The assessments identify a range of instructional needs and can be repeated over time to document children's growth. They are designed to take a short amount of time while giving the teacher a great deal of information about each child.

Assessing Children at Work
Teachers will benefit greatly from the data gathered from individual interviews, as it helps them know what to look for when they watch their students at work. The student interview gives teachers the information and insights into their children's thinking that enable them to focus right away on how the child approaches a task and easily interpret what they see. They are then able to respond immediately with appropriate support and challenges. What they observe then adds to the information gained from the interview, making their observations much more productive than they would otherwise be.

Taking Time for the Assessments
It is vitally important that teachers devote the time it takes to assess the instructional needs of their students. The data gathered through the student interviews is focused on foundational understandings that cannot be obtained in any other way and supplies the information necessary for teachers to provide the most focused and appropriate instruction possible. The assessments have been carefully designed to yield a great deal of information in the least amount of time.

It is reassuring to those who are giving the assessments for the first time to know that the time devoted to doing the assessments will lessen with familiarity with the assessments. Once teachers become familiar with the assessments, they will be able to find where the children are on a continuum of learning and will see it is not always necessary to go through the whole assessment with each child. The assessment is complete as soon as the teacher has reached the point in the assessment that identifies the edge of the child's understanding.

The power inherent in these assessments is that they are simple to administer but what can be learned from them is complex. The explanation of each assessment and description of what can be learned can take many pages, but the actual assessment can be done quickly and efficiently.

Teachers have found many different ways to accommodate their need to work with individual students. Sometimes they assess while the other children explore math materials, do quiet work such as reading or drawing, or have an assistant or parent helper read to them. Once the teacher has found a way to get this valuable information about each child, he or she sees that nothing else they might provide for the class is more important to the instructional program as a whole than gathering the information they need to provide appropriate instruction for their students.

Using the Assessment Forms

The assessment forms have been carefully crafted to help teachers pinpoint exactly where a child is on a continuum of understanding. The indicators are included on the form to help teachers know exactly what they are looking for and to minimize the amount of writing that will be necessary. Using the form may seem cumbersome at first, but with practice, teachers will become familiar with what they are looking for, the pattern of responses, and the layout of the form itself. Resist the temptation not to use the form, as that will just delay becoming familiar with the format and will make the assessment process less focused and clear.

Getting Authentic Information from the Student Interview

The essential value of the student interview is the insight teachers can get into the child's thinking, so it is important that the setting be conducive to getting authentic responses from the children. To ensure that the interview yields the most valid information possible, it is important for teachers not to give the children support to do the tasks. The teacher's attitude needs to be one of respectful listening and acceptance of wherever the children are in their understanding of mathematics. The interview should be considered an opportunity to gather information without judgment, and it is important that teachers not make evaluative comments, including praise. The information obtained will then allow teachers to provide their students with appropriate instruction.

Using the Assessments for Classroom Instruction

Because number concepts develop in relatively predictable ways, there are particular concepts and Critical Learning Phases that the majority of children at specific grade levels need to work with. Teachers can use these assessments to determine the instructional needs of the children along a continuum as they develop competence with these particular concepts. The following Grade Level charts provide guidance for teachers who are going to use the assessments to plan appropriate instruction for the whole class as they focus on various concepts throughout the year.

PRE-KINDERGARTEN		
Concepts	**Assessment Plans**	**Assessments**
Counting Objects	**Begin the year** by determining the number of objects the children can count. **Reassess** throughout the year, adapting the numbers as the children are able to count larger groups	**Assessment 1: Counting Objects** Begin with smaller numbers: use 12, 7, and 4 as the range of numbers and adjust according to the children's responses.
Beginning Number Relationships	**Later in the year,** if you have children who can count 12 or more objects with ease and accuracy, assess their ability to work with **number relationships.**	**Assessment 2: Changing Numbers** Focus primarily on using smaller numbers as assessed in the Going Back section.
Identifying and Combining Parts	**From the middle to the end of the year,** check to see if any of the children are beginning to **recognize small groups.**	**Assessment 4: Number Arrangements** Focus primarily on the recognition of small groups as assessed in the Going Back section.

KINDERGARTEN		
Concepts	**Assessment Plans**	**Assessments**
Counting Objects	**Begin the year** by determining the largest number of objects the children are able to count. **Reassess** throughout the year to check children's growth in facility with counting.	**Assessment 1: Counting Objects**
Beginning Number Relationships	**Once** children can count 20 or more objects with ease and accuracy, determine if they can see relationships between numbers.	**Assessment 2: Changing Numbers**
Identifying and Combining Parts	**Around the middle of the year,** check to see which children are able to recognize small groups of numbers and are beginning to see the parts of numbers.	**Assessment 4: Number Arrangements**
Decomposing Numbers to 10	**Towards the end of the year,** determine which children are able to decompose numbers. This is a challenging concept for many kindergarten children. There may be some children you want to assess earlier, but most children will not need to be given this assessment until late spring.	**Assessment 6: The Hiding Assessment**

FIRST GRADE		
Concepts	**Assessment Plans**	**Assessments**
Counting Objects *Beginning Number Relationships*	**Begin the year** by determining what foundational skills are in place. First check to see whether the children can count objects with ease and accuracy and whether they know one more and one less without counting. Also check to see whether the children are seeing relationships between numbers.	**Assessment 1: Counting Objects** **Assessment 2: Changing Numbers**
Comparing Numbers	**After several weeks**, expand the information you have about the children's understanding of numbers and number relationships by assessing their ability to compare numbers.	**Assessment 3: More/Less Trains**
Identifying and Combining Parts	**As you move to a focus on basic facts**, check the children's ability to identify and describe parts of numbers.	**Assessment 4: Number Arrangements**
Number Combinations *Decomposing Numbers to 10*	**Later,** assess the children's knowledge of number combinations. **Reassess** during the next several weeks to check for progress.	**Assessment 5: Combination Trains** **Assessment 6: The Hiding Assessment**
One Ten and Some More	**Towards the end of the year,** as you begin to work with tens and ones, determine whether the children are able to think of numbers as composed of one ten and some ones.	**Assessment 7: Ten Frames**
Numbers as Tens and Ones	**When you begin work with place value,** determine what children understand about numbers as tens and ones.	**Assessment 8: Grouping Tens**

SECOND GRADE		
Concepts	**Assessment Plan**	**Assessments**
Number Combinations *Decomposing Numbers to 10* *Comparing Numbers*	**Begin the year** by checking the children's knowledge of basic facts and their ability to compare numbers.	**Assessment 5: Combinations Trains** **Assessment 6: The Hiding Assessment** **Assessment 3: More/Less Trains**
Beginning Number Relationships *Identifying and Combining Parts*	**Meanwhile**, if you have children who are not proficient with basic facts or comparing numbers, check their abilities to see number relationships and parts of numbers.	**Assessment 2: Changing Numbers** **Assessment 4: Number Arrangements**
One Ten and Some More	**During the next few weeks,** check the children's ability to work with numbers as one ten and some more.	**Assessment 7: Ten Frames**
Numbers as Tens and Ones	**Later,** when you begin work with place value concepts, check children's understanding of numbers as tens and ones.	**Assessment 8: Grouping Tens**
Combining and Separating Tens and Ones	**Towards the end of the year,** assess the children's ability to combine and separate tens and ones when doing two-digit addition and subtraction.	**Assessment 9: Two-Digit Addition and Subtraction**

THIRD GRADE		
Concepts	**Assessment Plans**	**Assessments**
Use these assessments early in the school year to determine what foundational skills the children bring to third grade.		
Combining and Separating Tens and Ones	**Begin the year** by checking the children's ability to add and subtract two-digit numbers.	**Assessment 9: Two-Digit Addition and Subtraction**
If the children have difficulty making or breaking up tens, use the following assessments until you have determined what the children know, and what they still need to learn.		
Numbers as Tens and Ones	**Check** their understanding of numbers as tens and ones, and their ability to add and subract numbers to 20.	**Assessment 8: Grouping Tens** **Assessment 7: Ten Frames**
Decomposing Numbers	**Also,** assess their knowledge of parts of numbers.	**Assessment 6: The Hiding Assessment**
In a few weeks, reassess to see what progress has been made.		

Using the Assessments for Interventions

This series of assessments can be used to identify the needs of individual students who are having difficulty with the mathematics the rest of the class is working on. When assessing an individual student, the goal is to find the "edge of the child's understanding" in order to provide appropriate instruction that can build on what the child already knows. Often a child needs prerequisite skills to prepare him or her for instruction with the concept the class is working with. The following charts suggest a place to start for each grade level Pre-K through Grade 3. The key is to move between assessments until it has been determined what the child knows and can do and what the child still needs to learn.

Pre-Kindergarten

If the child is having difficulty learning to count objects:

Use **Counting Objects (Assessment 1)**.
Check the child's ability to count a small group of objects. Also check to see if the child can "hand you" a particular number of objects taken from a larger group. Begin with smaller numbers than indicated in the assessment. Begin with up to 8 objects and make the numbers smaller if necessary until the child is successful.

If the child is unable to count 2 or 3 objects, check the child's ability to match objects one-on-one. Suggestions for the kind of activity that will help you assess this idea can be found in *Developing Number Concepts: Book 1 Counting, Comparing and Pattern*. See Activity 1-23: Cover the Dots on page 53, and 1-24: Counting with the Number Shapes on page 54.

Kindergarten

If the child is having difficulty learning to count objects:

Use **Counting Objects (Assessment 1)**.
Begin with smaller numbers than indicated in the assessment. Start with 12 objects and make the numbers smaller if necessary until the child is successful.

If the child is able to count 12 objects sucessfully, ask him or her to count a pile of 21 objects.

If the child is unable to count 3 or 4 objects, check the child's ability to match objects one-on-one. Suggestions for the kind of activity that will help you assess this idea can be found in *Developing Number Concepts: Book 1 Counting, Comparing and Pattern*. See Activity 1-23: Cover the Dots on page 53, and 1-24: Counting with the Number Shapes on page 54.

First Grade

If the child is having difficulty counting and/or comparing numbers:

Use **Changing Numbers (Assessment 2)**.
Check to see if the child recognizes that one number is contained in another number and can change one number to another.

If it becomes evident through the Changing Numbers assessment that the child is not counting with ease and facility, check his or her ability to count.
Use **Counting Objects (Assessment 1)**.

If the child is having difficulty learning addition and subtraction facts:

Find out if the child is able to recognize and describe parts of numbers.
Use **Number Arrangements (Assessment 4)**.

If the child is not able to describe parts of numbers, check his or her understanding of the relationships between numbers by using **Changing Numbers (Assessment 2)**.

If the child is able to describe parts of numbers, check his or her understanding of number combinations using **Combination Trains (Assessment 5)** and **The Hiding Assessment (Assessment 6).**

Second or Third Grade

If the child is having difficulty learning basic addition and subtraction facts:

Check to see whether the child knows any number combinations without counting. Use **Combination Trains (Assessment 5)** and **The Hiding Assessment (Assessment 6)**.

If the child counts to find the total for most of the combinations or is unable to tell the missing parts of numbers larger than 3 or 4, check the child's ability to recognize and describe parts of numbers and his or her ability to recognize small groups without counting. Use **Number Arrangements (Assessment 4).**

If the child is having difficulty comparing numbers or solving comparative subtraction problems:

Determine his or her level of understanding of comparing by using **More/Less Trains (Assessment 3)**.

If comparing numbers is not easy for the child, also check the child's knowledge of particular relationships between numbers by using **Changing Numbers (Assessment 2).**

If the child is having difficulty understanding place value concepts:

Check the child's ability to think of numbers as composed of tens and ones by using **Grouping Tens (Assessment 8)**.

If necessary, check the child's idea of numbers as one ten and leftovers using the Going Back section of the Numbers as Tens and Ones assessment as well as **Ten Frames (Assessment 7)**.

If the child is having difficulty working with addition and subtraction of two-digit numbers:

Check the child's knowledge of number combinations to 10 using **The Hiding Assessment (Assessment 6)**. And also check the child's ability to think of numbers as composed of tens and ones by using **Grouping Tens (Assessment 8)**.

If the child can think of numbers as composed of tens and ones, check his or her ability to add and subtract teen numbers using **Ten Frames (Assessment 7)**.

If the child can make one ten and break apart one ten with ease, check his or her ability to work with several tens and ones using **Two-Digit Addition and Subtraction (Assessment 9)**.

GROUPING TENS ASSESSMENT

Assessment Eight

GROUPING TENS ASSESSMENT

LEARNING ABOUT NUMBERS AS TENS AND ONES

The term "place value" is used to refer to many different and complex ideas. In this chapter, we are focusing on one aspect of place value: namely, that numbers to 100 are composed of groups of tens and ones. The difficulty of this idea for young children has not always been recognized, and many teachers have made the assumption that children have learned place value concepts simply because they can use the language of tens and ones to label the digits in a number. Children must know more than what digit is in the tens place and which digit is in the ones place. They must understand that the underlying structure of the number is based on organizing numbers into groups of tens and ones. The goals that identify what children must know and understand about numbers as tens and ones, along with the related Critical Learning Phases that are crucial to the development of these understandings, are listed below and will be assessed through the tools presented in this chapter.

The Goals

CHILDREN NEED TO LEARN:
- That numbers to 100 are organized into groups of tens and ones
- To add tens without counting
- To take away tens without counting
- That counting by groups does not change the total quantity

Critical Learning Phases
- Organizes quantities into tens and ones
- Instantly knows total quantity when number of tens and ones is known
- Knows 10 more for any two-digit number
- Knows 10 less for any two-digit number

The Challenges of Learning to Think of Numbers as Tens and Ones

As children develop an understanding of number concepts, they move through many stages, often invisible to adults. Young children first understand quantities as one and one more and one more and so on. Over time, they begin to see relationships between quantities, and eventually they recognize that numbers are composed of parts. The next major idea that children must grapple with as they develop an understanding of number concepts is that groups can be counted as though they were single objects. This requires children to hold two ideas simultaneously. They must think of a group as one entity and as a collection at the same time. That is, they must understand that ten is both one ten and ten ones. This level of thinking is difficult for young children.

When the complexity of the ideas inherent in place value concepts are overlooked and children are deprived of the opportunity to make sense of the work they are asked to do in primary grades, their confusion persists as they move through school. Teachers of children in intermediate grades and middle school report that place value is still a difficult idea for many of their students. Children's long-term confusion begins when they are asked to work with place value concepts without the prerequisite understandings necessary in order to think of numbers as groups of tens and ones.

Teachers are often surprised at their children's responses when they ask questions that go beyond naming place values to using these ideas, as shown in the following examples.

Mrs. Huisman's kindergartners marked each day of school by adding a straw to a can labeled "Ones" and, whenever possible, making and placing bundles of tens into a can labeled "Tens." The class was very successful at repeating the right number of tens and ones when Mrs. Huisman asked them to. One day, she asked the children to tell how many straws there were in one of the bundles that they had named a "ten." Much to Mrs. Huisman's surprise, the children offered a variety of guesses. For them, the label "ten" was the name of the bundle rather than the number of straws.

Mrs. Stenberg's class of 5- and 6-year-olds had been recording the number of days they had been in school each morning since the school year began. On the 57th day, Mrs. Stenberg addressed the class, "Yesterday we had been in school 56 days. How many days have we been in school counting today?" The class responded, "57!" "How do we write fifty-seven?" she asked. "Five tens and seven ones," the children said as Mrs. Stenberg wrote 57. Later that day, Fern's mother brought in 36 cupcakes to celebrate Fern's birthday. Mrs. Stenberg told the class that Fern's mother told her there were 36 cupcakes and posed a question, "How many groups of ten do you think we could make with these 36 cupcakes?" Much to her surprise, the children had quite a variety of ideas: "I think 6 tens." "8 tens." "I think 4 tens." Mrs. Stenberg reminded them of what they already knew about tens and ones by asking them, "How would we write thirty-six?" Without hesitation, the class chorused, "3 tens and 6 ones." However, saying the number of tens and ones did not lead the children to change their minds about the number of groups of ten they could get with 36 cupcakes. They saw no connection between describing how to write a number and this real life situation. Mrs. Stenberg was reminded that children often use words correctly without fully understanding the concepts they are referring to.

When Mrs. Hinojos asked her first-graders to organize a bag of peanuts into groups of ten, the children found they had 8 groups of ten with 6 left over. After asking them to tell how many tens and how many ones they had, Mrs. Hinojos asked, "How many is that all together?" She intended to help the children count by tens to determine the total. Before she could begin to model this, several little hands reached for the tubs of ten peanuts and dumped them out so they could "really" count them to find out the actual number. This reminded Mrs. Hinojos of other situations where the children counted one by one. She remembered them counting each straw or pencil on their workbook pages even when they were pictured in bundles of 10.

Children have difficulty knowing which actions result in a change to the total number of a quantity and which actions do not. Knowing when the quantity stays the same is referred to as conservation of number. At a certain stage of thinking, children think the quantity changes if it is counted by twos or fives. They also lose track of the total quantity when regrouping. Lee Ann organized her connecting cubes into 3 tens and 2 ones. When she broke up one of the tens and put it with the ones, she was asked to tell how many she had all together. She thought she now had 42 and was shocked when she checked and found she still had 32. She had focused on adding to the ones, but did not realize she had simultaneously taken away from the sets of ten.

If we are to help children build an understanding of place value concepts, it is important that we find out what they are really thinking and understanding and not be misled when they can correctly label the tens and ones. It is only by knowing what the children think that we can provide them with the kinds of experiences that will help them develop a true understanding of the underlying structure of the numbers.

Another important idea that children must understand as they work with numbers as tens and ones is that the numerals used to write these numbers represent groups or individual objects depending on their place in the number. This can also be difficult for children if they do not understand the underlying structure of the numbers. For example, when Saul's teacher asked him to show 34 with connecting cubes, he put out three cubes and four cubes. It is useful to note that the misconception evident in this situation can be perpetuated if we ask children to count dimes without understanding that the dime represents a group of ten but cube does not.

The Assessment Tools

Four sections in this guide describe the materials that will help teachers assess children's understanding of numbers as tens and ones. The first section, "The Student Interview," provides needed information for using the forms for the assessment, "Grouping Tens." The next section, "Meeting Instructional Needs," offers help in organizing this assessment information on the Class Summary sheets and provides guidelines for appropriate instruction. The following section, "Assessing Children at Work," describes how to monitor children's progress while at work using the task "Measuring Shapes." The last section, "Linking Assessment and Instruction," directs teachers to resources so they can provide instruction to meet the identified needs.

THE STUDENT INTERVIEW

If teachers want to determine what children know about numbers as tens and ones, they must do more than ask them to name the digits in a number. They need to see how they use the idea of tens and ones to determine how many. The student interview is a focused way to gather the information you need to provide appropriate ongoing instruction. Before using the student interview to assess the children, become familiar with the structure of the assessment and the indicators used to document children's growth.

The indicators specific to each area being assessed identify the particular level of facility that the children have reached. They are organized into categories that describe the kind of instruction the children need, and thus they help teachers interpret what the children have learned. The category "Ready to Apply" means that the child can already do the particular task and is ready to use this skill in other settings. The category "Needs Practice" indicates that the child can do a particular task with some level of effort but still needs more experiences in order to develop facility and consistency. The third category, "Needs Instruction," covers the kinds of responses that show the child is not yet able to do the task.

S.I. THE STUDENT INTERVIEW: GROUPING TENS

The student interview "Grouping Tens" is designed primarily to determine whether children know the total number of a quantity when they know the number of tens and ones. In Part One, the teacher presents children with 34 connecting cubes. The children are asked to estimate the total number of cubes and then the number of groups of ten they think they can make. The children are requested to organize the cubes into tens and ones to see whether they can determine the total number of objects when they know the number of tens and ones. They are then asked how many there would be if 10 were added to 34 and how many there would be if 10 were removed from 34. If the children know 10 more and 10 less without counting, they are asked questions to determine whether they can add and subtract 20 and whether they can add 12 to 7 tens. If they are unable to use the groups of ten to help them determine the total number of cubes, they are asked to tell the number of leftovers in 17. In Part Two of the interview, the children are asked how many cubes there would be if they were counted by fives. They then count the group of objects by fives. This same procedure is followed for counting by twos.

This assessment is designed to identify instructional needs for children working at ability levels ranging from counting by ones (even when the cubes are organized into groups of tens) to knowing 10 more and 10 less than a number if the total number of tens and ones is known. The extension identifies those children who can add and subtract 20 and can add 12 to 7 tens without counting. It also identifies instructional needs for children who are unable to count by twos and/or fives to those who count by twos and fives with ease.

The chart below is intended to help you become familiar with the structure of the student interview before you work with the actual recording sheets. It outlines the steps you will follow and the questions you will ask. On the next three pages are examples of actual interviews, which will give you an idea of what you might expect when giving this assessment to children. Following are copies of the actual recording forms, including the indicators. A step-by-step explanation of each section of the recording form and indicators follows each page of the interview.

"Grouping Tens"

Looking at the Structure of the Student Interview

PART ONE: Organizing into Tens and Ones
Present the child with a pile of **34** connecting cubes. Ask: *"How many do you think there might be?"* *"How many groups of tens do you think you can make?"*
Say: *"Check and see how many tens you can make."* *"How many groups of ten did you make?"* *"How many leftovers?"* *"Does this give you an idea of how many there are?"* If the child does not respond with the total quantity, ask, *"Can you find out?"*
Push the cubes back into a pile and ask, *"Now, how many are there?"*
Choose the appropriate column below.

GOING BACK If the child determined the quantity by counting by ones, ask the following:	**GOING ON** If the child counted by tens or knew the quantity without counting, ask the following:
Remove some cubes, leaving a pile of 17, and ask the child to find out *"How many?"* Then ask: *"How many trains of ten do you think you can make?"* *"Go ahead and make a train."* As the child makes a train of ten, ask: *"How many leftovers do you think there will be?"*	*"How many will there be if we add 10 more?"* *"What if we take 10 away?"*
Put back the cubes previously removed (to end up with 34) and go on to page 2.	If the child adds and subtracts 10 without counting, ask the following questions. (If they counted to get the answer, skip these questions and go on to page 2.)

	EXTENSION
	"What if we
	    ...added 20 more?
	    ...took 20 away?
	    ...had 7 tens and we added 12 more?"

PART TWO: Conservation and Counting by Groups
"If we counted these cubes by fives, how many would there be?" *"Would you check and see?"*
"If we counted these cubes by twos, how many would there be?" *"Would you check and see?"*

Examples of the Student Interview

(allow 2-8 minutes per child)

The following examples of student interviews give you a picture of what you might expect during the interview and will help make the detailed description found on the following pages more meaningful.

TORY:

Who is Tory? Tory could be a second grader who is making good progress in understanding tens and ones, or he could be a third grader who is beginning to make sense of the numbers he worked with the year before.

Mr. Karl presents Tory with a pile of 34 connecting cubes and asks, "How many do you think there are?" Tory hesitates and then says, "20." Mr. Karl then says, "If there are 20, how many groups of ten do you think you can make?" "2," Tory replies. "Check and see how many tens you can make," Mr. Karl directs. Tory makes two piles of ten and then says, "It can't be 20. I already have 20 and there's still more. Maybe it will be about 30." Tory forms all the groups of ten he can and ends up with 3 tens and 4 extra. Mr. Karl asks, "How many groups of ten did you make?" "3," Tory says. "And how many leftovers?" asks Mr. Karl. "4," Tory says. "Does this give you an idea of how many there are?" Mr. Karl asks. "There's 34," Tory says. Mr. Karl pushes the cubes back into a pile and asks, "Now, how many are there?" "Still 34," says Tory. "How do you know?" Mr. Karl asks. Tory replies, "Because you didn't do anything. It's still the same."

At this point in the assessment, Mr. Karl has to make a choice between going back to easier questions or on to more challenging questions. He recognizes that Tory is ready for a more difficult question, so he goes on. He asks, "How many will there be if we add 10 more?" "If you had another 10 you would have 4 tens so that would be 44," Tory replies. Mr. Karl then asks, "What if we had 34 and we took 10 away?" Tory takes a minute to think about this. "Oh yeah, you would just have 2 tens so it would be 24."

Since Tory can add and subtract 10 without counting, Mr. Karl goes on to the extension questions. "What if we added 20 more?" he asks. Tory says, "Well, 10 more would be 44 and another ten would be 54." "What if we had 34 and we took 20 away?" Mr. Karl asks. Tory takes a long time to answer. After he says, "14." Mr. Karl asks, "How did you figure that out?" Tory says, "I was thinking of the piles we had before. If we had 3 tens and I took one away, that would be 2 tens, but we took another ten away, so that would be 1 ten and 4 left. That's 14." Next Mr. Karl asks, "What if we had 7 tens and we added 12 more?" Tory says, "7 tens is 70. 71, 72, 73, 74, 75, 76, 77," he continues counting until he gets to 82. "It's 82," he says.

Mr. Karl sees that Tory can count on by tens and visualizes the groups of ten to take 20 away, but when the numbers are larger than he can think about at this point, he counts on to add.

He goes on to Part Two of the interview. "If we counted these cubes by fives, how many would there be?" Tory smiles and asks, "What do you mean?" Mr. Karl says, "There's no trick here. I just want to know if you know how many there would be if we counted these by fives." "It's still going to be 34," Tory says. "Would you count these by fives and show me?" Mr. Karl asks. He has learned that Tory does not think the number will change, but he still wants to see how Tory counts by fives. Tory is able to count five at a time easily and ends up with 34. "If we counted these cubes by twos, how many would there be?" asks Mr. Karl. "Still the same," Tory says. "Would you count these by twos and let me see?" Tory begins counting by twos with ease but when he gets to 12, he hesitates just a bit for each number until he gets to 20 and finds it easy again. Mr. Karl sees that Tory has a strong sense of numbers as tens and ones and is ready to work more on using this knowledge to develop facility adding and subtracting.

SIERRA:

Who is Sierra? Sierra could be a first grader who is not yet able to think of numbers as tens and ones or a second grader who is struggling with the concept.

Mrs. Frese places 34 connecting cubes on the table in front of Sierra and asks, "How many do you think there are?" Sierra looks at the pile and says, "20." "If there are 20, how many groups of ten do you think you could make?" Mrs. Frese asks. "Well, probably 3 or 2," Sierra says as she begins arranging the cubes into groups. She ends up with 3 groups of ten with 4 leftover. "How many tens did you make?" asks Mrs. Frese. "3 tens," Sierra replies. "And how many leftovers?" Mrs. Frese asks. "4," replies Sierra. Mrs. Frese continues, "Does that give you an idea of how many all together?" "Hmmmm," Sierra says. "It's not 20. 10 and 10 is 20. Probably . . . I don't know." Mrs. Frese asks, "Is there a way for you to find out?" "I know that 10 and 10 is 20." Sierra says and begins counting the remaining cubes by ones, saying "21, 22," and so forth. As she counts, she misses a couple of cubes and ends up with 32. "It's 32," she tells Mrs. Frese. Mrs. Frese notes that Sierra does not see any relationship between the number of tens and ones and the total and thus is unaware that she may have made a mistake when she counted.

Mrs. Frese decides to ask Sierra the question under the Going Back section of the assessment before going on to page 2 of the assessment. She removes some of the cubes, leaving 17. "Would you count this pile?" she asks. After Sierra has counted the pile, Mrs. Frese asks, "How many trains of 10 do you think you could make with this pile? "I could make one train," Sierra says. "Go ahead and make a train," she directs. While Sierra is putting the connecting cubes together, Mrs. Frese asks, "Do you know how many leftovers you are going to have?" Sierra stops and thinks, "I think it is going to be 6 left," she says. "How were you thinking about that?" Mrs. Frese asks. "Well, I was counting to 17 and I ended up with 6 left." Again Sierra shows she does not see the relationship between the number of leftovers and the total number of cubes. Since she is not yet able to decompose 17 into 1 ten and 7 leftovers, Mrs. Frese will work with her focusing on that idea to support her work with tens and ones. Mrs. Frese puts the cubes she removed earlier back into the pile and asks Sierra if she remembers how many cubes are in the pile. "I think 32," she says. Mrs. Frese decides not to ask Sierra to recount the cubes before asking the next question. "You told me before that there were 32. How many do you think there would be if we counted them by fives?" "I don't know. That could be a lot," Sierra responds. "What do you *think* it could be?" Mrs. Frese restates the question, emphasizing she is just asking Sierra what it might be. "55?" Sierra says quietly. "Would you check?" Mrs. Frese asks. Sierra then begins to move one cube at a time saying, "5, 10, 15, 20," until she gets to 100. "I only know up to 100," she says. Mrs. Frese sees that Sierra doesn't understand what it means to count by fives, but she goes on to the next question about counting by twos just to see what Sierra will do in this situation. "How many do you think there would be if you counted these by twos?" "I think it could be 40," Sierra says. "Would you check and see?" Mrs. Frese asks. "Okay," Sierra says as she begins to count. Sierra again moves one at a time, this time saying, "2,4,6,8,10." When she gets to 10, she hesitates a bit and says 11 under her breath and then 12 out loud. She continues in this way until she gets to 20. Beginning with 20, she is confident again and counts "22, 24, 26, 28, 30," ending at 68.

Mrs. Frese makes note that Sierra does not understand the idea that a number is composed of tens and ones and that she does not understand what counting by groups means.

"Grouping Tens"

Concept 8: Numbers As Tens And Ones　　　　　　　　*Student Interview*

S.I.	◁ p.1
C.S.	
A.W.	

YOU NEED:	GOAL:	PROCEDURE:
34 connecting cubes, all one color	To determine if the child can tell "how many" in a quantity if the number of tens and ones is known and to determine if the child can add ten and take away ten without counting.	Present the child with 34 connecting cubes. Ask the questions below and circle the indicators for each question.

PART ONE: ORGANIZING INTO TENS AND ONES

PRESENT THE CHILD WITH 34 CONNECTING CUBES

Ask:
"*How many do you think there might be?*"　　　_____ Doesn't estimate　　　Estimates: _____

Ask:
"*How many groups of ten do you think you can make?*"　　Says: _____

NUMBER OF TENS IN A NUMBER	
I	Tens and ones not related to the estimate
A	Tells correct number of tens

Say: "*Check and see how many tens you can make.*" (piles, not trains)

While the child is counting out tens, notice and mark child's reaction and/or new estimate.

REACTION TO ESTIMATE	
I	No reaction
P	Reacts, no new estimate
A	Spontaneously makes new estimate

After the child has made all the tens possible, ask: "*How many groups of ten did you make?*" "*How many leftovers?*"　　Tens_____　Leftovers_____

Ask: "*Does this give you an idea of how many there are?*" If necessary, ask: "*Can you find out?*"　　Says: _____

DETERMINES QUANTITY	
I	Counts all by ones
P	Count by tens, and then counts the ones
A	Knows the total quantity without needing to count

● If the child counted all by ones, ask the following question and then use the **Going Back** column.
● If the child counted by tens or knew the quantity without counting, ask the following question and use the **Going On** column.

Push the cubes back into a pile and ask: "*Now, how many are there? ...How do you know?*"　　Says: _____

GOING BACK			GOING ON		
Remove some cubes, leaving a pile of 17. Ask the child to find out "*How many are in this pile?*" Ask: "*How many trains of ten do you think you can make?*" "*Go ahead and make a train.*"	Says:		"*How many will there be if we add 10 more?*"	Says:	**PLUS 10** I Guesses or gets wrong answer P Figures out A Knows without counting
As the child begins to make a train of ten, ask, "*How many leftovers do you think there will be?*"	Says:	**ONE TEN AND LEFTOVERS** I Guesses or gets wrong answer P Figures out accurately A- Knows, but checks A Knows without counting	"*What if we take 10 away?*" (refocus on 34 if necessary)	Says:	**MINUS 10** I Guesses or gets wrong answer P Figures out A Knows without counting
Put back the cubes previously removed. If necessary, remind the child that there are 34 and go on to page 2.			If the child adds and subtracts 10 without counting, ask the EXTENSION questions. (If the child counted to get the answers, skip these questions and go on to pg. 2.)		

EXTENSION: Use the indicators as above.

Say:		Says:	I	P	A		Says:	I	P	A
"*What if we...*	added 20 more?"					had 7 tens and we added 12 more?"				
	took 20 away?"									

SUMMARIZING INSTRUCTIONAL NEEDS

GOING BACK: ONE TEN AND LEFTOVERS		NUMBER OF TENS		DETERMINES QUANTITY		GOING ON	+10	-10
A A-	Knows without counting Knows, but checks	A	Tells the number of tens	A	Knows without counting	A Knows without counting		
P	Figures out accurately	I	Unable to tell the number of tens	P	Counts by tens	P Figures out		
I	Guesses or gets wrong answer			I	Counts by ones	I Guesses or gets wrong answer		

	+20			-20			7 TENS + 12		
EXTENSION:	I	P	A	I	P	A	I	P	A

© Kathy Richardson. Mathematical Perspectives, Publisher, P.O. Box 29418, Bellingham, WA 98228-9418. 360-715-2782. www.mathperspectives.com Reproduction of this page in any form is prohibited. To order assessment forms, contact publisher

34

Concept 8: Student Interview Form Page 1 of 2

Understanding the Recording Form and Indicators

Look at the Student Interview form on the adjoining page. In the upper right-hand corner is a picture of connecting cubes, with some arranged into a group of ten. This identifies the set of assessments for Concept 8: Numbers as Tens and Ones. Look for the shaded S.I. box indicating that this is a Student Interview form. The following is a step-by-step explanation of each section of the form. Because this particular assessment has two pages, you will notice a special page symbol indicating this is page one of the assessment. ⟨p. 1

Part One: Organizing Into Tens and Ones

In this assessment, you ask a series of questions that will give you information about the child's ability to think of numbers as tens and ones. Read each question, record the child's responses, and circle the appropriate indicators. In this particular assessment, each question has its own set of indicators that are described following each section of the assessment.

✂ SECTION 1:

Present the child with 34 connecting cubes and ask him or her to make an estimate. Some children will hesitate or start to count. If this is the case, reassure them that it is just a guess. You want to encourage them to make an estimate because the next question, "How many groups of ten do you think can you make?" is based on the number they give as an estimate.

Ask: "How many do you think there are?"
"How many groups of tens do you think you can make?"

PART ONE: ORGANIZING INTO TENS AND ONES		
PRESENT THE CHILD WITH 34 CONNECTING CUBES		
Ask: *"How many do you think there might be?"*	_____ Doesn't estimate Estimates: _____	
Ask: *"How many groups of ten do you think you can make?"*	Says:	**NUMBER OF TENS IN A NUMBER**
		I Tens and ones not related to the estimate A Tells correct number of tens

When children make an estimate, it gives you an idea of what they think a large number is. The most common estimate made by first and second graders happens to be the number "20."

Children often learn to label the number in the tens place without knowing what it actually means. We can get a glimpse into their understanding of numbers as tens and ones by asking them to tell the number of groups of ten they could make if their estimate were the actual number.

THE INDICATORS FOR NUMBER OF TENS IN A NUMBER

Needs Instruction (I)

(I) Tens and ones not related to the estimate
At this stage, the children do not think of numbers as tens and ones, so they don't see the connection between the number of tens in their estimate and the number of tens they expect to make.

Ready to Apply (A)

(A) Tens and ones match estimate
At this stage, the children do see the connection between the number estimated and the number of tens they expect to make. So, for example, if they estimated 30, they would predict they could make 3 tens.

✄ SECTION 2:

In this section, you ask the children to see how many tens they can make. Even though you are using connecting cubes, ask the children not to connect the cubes into sticks of ten. This is because we want to find out if they can think of a group of ten single objects as one entity even if they are not joined. Making ten sticks is a valuable way to learn to think of numbers as tens and ones, but in this assessment, we want to check the children's ability to think in tens and ones without that structure to aid their thinking. While they are making groups of ten, notice whether they spontaneously react to or change their estimate. Circle the appropriate indicator.

Ask: "Check and see how many tens you can make."

Say: **"Check and see how many tens you can make."** (piles, not trains)		
		REACTION TO ESTIMATE
While the child is counting out tens, notice and mark child's reaction and/or new estimate.	I	No reaction
	P	Reacts, no new estimate
	A	Spontaneously makes new estimate

> Children who are just beginning to work with groups of tens and ones have not yet developed a strong sense of quantity for these large numbers, so most will not react to the estimate. However, the lack of a reaction, in and of itself, gives us valuable information about the meaning the numbers have for them.

THE INDICATORS FOR REACTION TO ESTIMATE

Needs Instruction (I)

(I) No reaction
At this stage, the children are focused on making groups of ten and not on the total number, so they do not pay attention to whether their estimate is close or not.

Needs Practice (P)

(P) Reacts, no new estimate
At this stage, the children are aware of the quantity of the number they are working with, so they notice if they reach the number they estimated while forming groups of ten. However, they react only with a comment or hesitation and don't stop to make another estimate.

Ready to Apply (A)

(A) Spontaneously makes a new estimate
At this stage, the children make a new estimate while forming groups and are able to use some sense of the quantity to get closer. They might say something like, "I thought it would be 20 but I already have 2 tens and 2 more, and that is more than 20 already. It looks like I can only make about one more ten so I want to change my mind. Now I think it's going to be 30."

✂SECTION 3:

This section focuses on the central idea being assessed in this interview. Pay close attention to the way the children determine the total number of objects. The indicators list the most common approaches. Record the children's responses and circle the appropriate indicator.

Ask: "How many groups of ten did you make?"
"How many leftovers?"
"Does this give you an idea of how many there are?"

After the child has made all the tens possible, ask: *"How many groups of ten did you make?"* *"How many leftovers?"*		Tens____ Leftovers____
Ask: *"Does this give you an idea of how many there are?"* If necessary, ask: *"Can you find out?"*	Says:	**DETERMINES QUANTITY**
		I Counts all by ones P Count by tens and then counts the ones A Knows the total quantity without needing to count

THE INDICATORS FOR DETERMINES QUANTITY

Needs Instruction (I)

(I) Counts all by ones
At this stage, the children do not see numbers as tens and ones, so grouping them into tens and ones does not help them determine the total. The only strategy they understand how to use (to determine the total) is counting by ones.

If any of the children determine the total number by counting all the objects, ask them the question found in Section 4 and then choose the Going Back column. The questions in the Going Back section will help you determine whether the child understands how the teen numbers are structured. Understanding numbers as one ten and some more can be a precursor to understanding that numbers can be composed of several tens and more.

Needs Practice (P)

(P) Counts by tens and then counts the ones
At this stage, the children count the groups by tens to determine the total. Although this is a more advanced way of counting than counting all by ones, it indicates that the children do not yet see the relationship between the tens and ones and the total.

Ready to Apply (A)

(A) Knows the total quantity without needing to count.
At this stage, as soon as the children know the number of tens and ones, they automatically know the total without needing to count. How the children determine the total is the key piece of information in this assessment, because it indicates whether or not the children are able to think of numbers as tens and ones. This is based on whether or not they can immediately see the relationship between the number of tens and the total.

✂ SECTION 4: Ask the question below and write down the child's response.

**Push the cubes back into a pile and ask,
"Now, how many are there?"..."How do you know?"**

Push the cubes back into a pile and ask: *"Now, how many are there?"* ..."*How do you know?*"	Says:

There are two reasons for pushing the cubes back into a pile and asking the children to tell how many. One is to see whether the children know that the quantity has not changed. At a certain stage of thinking, children are not sure that the number is the same after it has been rearranged and will need to recount to find out. The children who think the number might have changed are said to lack conservation of number. Some children who do have conservation of number will think the answer is obvious and will wonder why you asked the question. They know the quantity is "conserved" even though the cubes have been changed (rearranged) in some way.

The second reason for pushing the cubes back together is so that they are not organized for the next question. This is to make sure the children do not have extra clues that mislead us into thinking they know more about tens and ones than they really do.

✂ SECTION 5: Going Back or Going On

At this point in the assessment, you will need to decide whether to have the children go back to an easier question or on to a more challenging one. If the child was unable to use the organization of tens and ones to help them determine the total number of cubes and had to count them all to find out how many, choose the questions in the Going Back column. If they were able to count by tens or tell the total without counting, choose the Going On column.

GOING BACK

Ask: "How many trains of ten can you make?"
"How many leftovers do you think there will be?"

GOING BACK			
Remove some cubes, leaving a pile of 17. Ask the child to find out **"How many are in this pile?"** Ask: **"How many trains of ten do you think you can make?"** **"Go ahead and make a train."**			Says:
As the child begins to make a train of ten, ask, **"How many leftovers do you think there will be?"**	Says:	I P A- A	**ONE TEN AND LEFTOVERS** Guesses or gets wrong answer Figures out accurately Knows, but checks Knows without counting
Put back the cubes previously removed. If necessary, remind the child there are 34 and go on to page 2.			

This question is designed to determine whether the child knows the number of leftovers when a number is decomposed into one ten and leftovers. Sometimes children have learned the patterns of tens and ones, and so know that 10 and 7 make 17 without really understanding the structure of the teen numbers well enough to answer correctly when asked to decompose rather than combine the numbers.

After you have asked the question and circled the appropriate indicator, put back the cubes previously removed so you end up with 34 cubes again and go on to page 2.

THE INDICATORS FOR ONE TEN AND LEFTOVERS (GOING BACK)

Needs instruction (I)

(I) Guesses or gets wrong answer
At this stage, the children just make a guess. Asking children, "What do you think?" will sometimes result in them guessing when they aren't sure, rather than saying they don't know. Sometimes, when the children don't know the number of leftovers, they count to find out. If they make an error and don't notice it, it is further evidence that they don't recognize the structure of 17 as 1 ten and 7.

Needs Practice (P)

(P) Figures out accurately
At this stage, the children can get the right answer but need to figure it out. Even when children figure out the answer correctly, the fact that they had to count is evidence that they don't understand the structure of the number as ten and some more.

Ready to Apply (A)

(A-) Knows, but needs to check
At this stage, the child is able to tell the number of leftovers without counting but is unsure for some reason. For some, it will be because they have not been asked the question in this way so they will need to check.

(A) Knows without counting
At this stage, the child knows the number of leftovers without counting. This indicates the child does understand the underlying structure of the number.

GOING ON

There are two questions in this section of the chart. First the child is asked to add 10 and then to take 10 away. Notice that the questions are posed as "What If?" type questions and that the children have no cubes to use to figure out the answer.

GOING ON		
"How many will there be if we add 10 more?"	Says:	**PLUS 10** I Guesses or gets wrong answer P Figures out A Knows without counting
"What if we take 10 away?" (refocus on 34 if necessary)	Says:	**MINUS 10** I Guesses or gets wrong answer P Figures out A Knows without counting
If the child adds and subtracts 10 without counting, ask the EXTENSION questions. (If they counted to get the answers, skip these questions and go on to pg. 2.)		

First Question: "How many will there be if we add 10 more?"

This is an important question to ask as a check of the children's ability to think of numbers as tens and ones. If the children know more than the pattern of tens and ones, they will be able to use their knowledge of tens and ones to add one more ten without needing to figure it out.

THE INDICATORS FOR PLUS TEN (GOING ON)

Needs Instruction (I)

(I) Guesses or gets wrong answer
This is a difficult problem for those children who do not yet see the structure of the numbers and who need models in order to figure the answer out correctly.

Needs Practice (P)

(P) Figures out
Some children will be able to add on 10, but from their perspective the 10 has no significance. Adding 10 is just like adding any other number. They aren't thinking in terms of the groups of tens and ones they formed earlier, or they would know without figuring it out.

Ready to Apply (A)

(A) Knows without counting
Some children will know instantly that adding one more ten will obviously mean there will be 4 tens and thus the answer is 44. They are using their understanding of the structure of numbers as tens and ones.

Second Question: "What if we take 10 away?"

This is one more check of the child's ability to think of numbers in terms of tens and ones. Although subtraction is generally harder, for some children this is easier because they visualize the 3 groups they just made and take one pile away. Other children will need to figure out the answer, which shows that they are not yet fully aware of the underlying structure of the numbers.

THE INDICATORS FOR MINUS TEN (GOING ON)

Needs Instruction (I)

(I) Guesses or gets wrong answer
It can be very difficult for children to subtract without the use of models if they cannot use the underlying structure of numbers as tens and ones.

Needs Practice (P)

(P) Figures out

Some children will be able to take 10 away, but, as was true for adding 10, the ten has no significance for them. Taking 10 away is just like taking away any other number.

Ready to Apply (A)

(A) Knows without counting

Some children will know instantly that taking one ten away means there will be 2 tens and thus the answer is 24. This indicates that they understand and can use their knowledge of the underlying structure of numbers as tens and ones.

✂ SECTION 6: Extension

Pose the following problems only if the child can add and subtract 10 without counting. Use the same indicators as used when adding and subtracting 10 as described above. Make note of whether or not the children use their knowledge of tens and ones in answering these questions. (If they counted when adding or taking away 10, skip these questions and go on to Part Two of the assessment on page 2.)

EXTENSION: Use the indicators as above.										
Say:		Says:	I	P	A		Says:	I	P	A
"What if we...	added 20 more?"					had 7 tens and we added 12 more?"				
	took 20 away?"									

✂ SECTION 7: Summarizing Instructional Needs for Part One

At the bottom of page 1 of the Student Interview form is a place to summarize what you have learned thus far. You will not want to stop to fill this out at this point in the assessment. Instead, finish giving the assessment that continues on the second page of this Student Interview form. After you have finished the assessment and have excused the child, you will have the information necessary to fill out the summary for both pages. A discussion of how to fill out the form will come at the end of the discussion of page 2 of this assessment.

SUMMARIZING INSTRUCTIONAL NEEDS										
GOING BACK: ONE TEN AND LEFTOVERS		**NUMBER OF TENS**		**DETERMINES QUANTITY**		**GOING ON**		**+10**	**-10**	
A Knows without counting **A-** Knows, but checks		**A** Tells the number of tens		**A** Knows without counting		**A** Knows without counting				
P Figures out accurately		**I** Unable to tell the number of tens		**P** Counts by tens		**P** Figures out				
I Guesses or gets wrong answer				**I** Counts by ones		**I** Guesses or gets wrong answer				
EXTENSION:		**+20**		**-20**		**7 TENS + 12**				
		I	P	A	I	P	A	I	P	A

Concept 8: Numbers As Tens And Ones　　　　　*Student Interview*

S.I. | p. 2
C.S.
A.W.

GOAL:
To determine if the child knows that the total number does not change when counted in a different way.
To determine if the child understands what it means to count by twos and fives and to find out how well they can do this.

PART TWO: CONSERVATION AND COUNTING BY GROUPS

Ask: *"If we counted these by fives, how many would there be?"*	Says:	CONSERVATION (when counting by fives)	
		I	Says a different number
		P	Ignores leftovers or restricts answer to a number that can be reached by counting by fives
		A	Says the correct number and explains thinking

Ask: *"Would you check and see?"*	Says:	COUNTING BY FIVES	
		I-	Counts each cube as 5, rote counting sequence inaccurate
		I	Counts each cube as 5, rote counting sequence accurate
		P	Counts by groups of 5, rote counting sequence inaccurate
		P+	Counts by groups of 5, rote counting sequence accurate but difficult
		A	Counts by groups of 5, accurately and easily

Ask: *"If we counted these by twos, how many would there be?"*	Says:	CONSERVATION (when counting by twos)	
		I	Says a different number
		P	If using an odd number of cubes, restricts answer to a number that can be reached by counting by twos
		A	Says the correct number and explains thinking

Ask: *"Would you check and see?"*	Says:	COUNTING BY TWOS	
		I-	Counts each cube as 2, rote counting sequence inaccurate
		I	Counts each cube as 2, rote counting sequence accurate
		P	Counts by groups of 2, rote counting sequence inaccurate
		P+	Counts by groups of 2, rote counting sequence accurate but difficult
		A	Counts by groups of 2, accurately and easily

SUMMARIZING INSTRUCTIONAL NEEDS

COUNTING BY FIVES				COUNTING BY TWOS			
CONSERVATION		COUNTING BY GROUPS		CONSERVATION		COUNTING BY GROUPS	
A	Says the correct number and explains thinking	A	Counts by groups with ease and accuracy	A	Says the correct number and explains thinking	A	Counts by groups with ease and accuracy
P	Ignores leftovers or restricts answer to a number that can be reached by counting by fives	P	Counts by groups, but rote sequence difficult	P	If using an odd number of cubes, restricts answer to a number that can be reached by counting by twos	P	Counts by groups, but rote sequence difficult.
I	Guesses a different number	I	Moves one at a time, but counts by groups	I	Guesses a different number	I	Moves one at a time, but counts by groups

© Kathy Richardson. Mathematical Perspectives, Publisher, P.O. Box 29418, Bellingham, WA 98228-9418. 360-715-2782. www.mathperspectives.com Reproduction of this page in any form is prohibited. To order assessment forms, contact publisher.

43

Understanding the Recording Form and Indicators

Look at the second page of the Student Interview Form on the preceding page. Look for the page 2 symbol located in the upper right-hand corner of the sheet. You can tell at glance that this is the second page of the assessment. The following is a step-by-step explanation of each section of the form.   ⟨p. 2

Part Two of this assessment includes questions that reveal the children's understanding of conservation of numbers and their understanding of and facility with counting by groups.

✂ SECTION 8:

In this section, you will check to see whether the children have conservation of large numbers when they are asked to think about how many there would be if they counted the pile of 34 by fives. This question is asked to find out whether the children realize that the quantity stays the same when objects are grouped or counted in a different way.

Ask: "If we counted these cubes by fives, how many would there be?"

PART TWO: CONSERVATION AND COUNTING BY GROUPS			
Ask: *"If we counted these by fives how many would there be?"*	Says:	**CONSERVATION (when counting by fives)**	
		I	Says a different number
		P	Ignores leftovers or restricts answer to a number that can be reached by counting by fives
		A	Says the correct number and explains thinking

Teachers are often very surprised to find that children really believe the quantity can change if they count it differently. This is natural as children develop an understanding of which processes change the quantity and which do not. When children do understand that the quantity does not change, the fact that the number has to be the same is so obvious to them they think the teacher must be asking them something else. So they interpret the question as though you were asking, "How many groups of five can you make?" If this appears to be the case, try to clarify the question for them by saying, "You're telling me how many groups of five. I want to know how many cubes there will be if we counted these by fives."

THE INDICATORS FOR CONSERVATION OF NUMBER

Needs Instruction (I)

(I) Says a different number
At this stage, children believe changing the way you count something will change the outcome.

Needs Practice (P)

(P) Ignores leftovers or restricts answer to a number that can be reached by counting by fives
At this stage, the child thinks that counting by fives requires you to land on a number ending with 0 or 5 and so ignores the extras when giving you an answer.

Ready to Apply (A)

(A) Says the correct number
At this stage, the child knows the quantity is not changed when counting by fives.

✂ SECTION 9:

Ask: "Would you check and see?"

Ask: "Would you check and see?"	Says:	COUNTING BY FIVES	
		I-	Counts each cube as 5, rote counting sequence inaccurate
		I	Counts each cube as 5, rote counting sequence accurate
		P	Counts by groups of 5, rote counting sequence inaccurate
		P+	Counts by groups of 5, rote counting sequence accurate but difficult
		A	Counts by groups of 5, accurately and easily

Having the children count the pile by fives provides the opportunity to find out whether the children understand what it means to count by fives and how well they can do this. Do not be surprised if some children have a misconception of what it means to count by fives and move one cube at a time while saying, "5, 10, 15, 20," and so forth.

THE INDICATORS FOR COUNTING BY GROUPS

Needs Instruction (I)

(I-) Counts each cube as 5, rote counting sequence inaccurate
At this stage, the children show they do not understand what it means to count by fives as they move one at a time instead of 5 at a time to count. In addition, they do not know the rote counting sequence.

(I) Counts each cube as 5, rote counting sequence accurate
In this case, the children do not understand what it means to count by fives as they move one at a time instead of 5 at a time to count. However, they do know the rote counting sequence.

Needs Practice (P)

(P) Counts by groups of 5, rote sequence inaccurate
In this case, the children understand what it means to count by fives but do not know the rote counting sequence.

(P+) Counts by groups of 5, rote sequence accurate, but difficult
In this case, the children understand what it means to count by fives but still have some difficulty with the rote counting sequence.

Ready to Apply (A)

(A) Counts by groups of 5 accurately and with ease
At this stage, the child knows what it means to count by fives and knows the rote counting sequence as well.

✂ SECTION 10

This section is exactly as above except that you are asking the children to count by twos. The rote sequence for counting by twos is much more difficult than the sequence for counting by fives so you may have more children having difficulty with that aspect of the assessment.

Ask: "If we counted these cubes by twos, how many would there be?" "Would you check and see?"

Ask: *"If we counted these by twos, how many would there be?"*	Says:	CONSERVATION (when counting by twos)	
		I	Says a different number
		P	If using an odd number of cubes, restricts answer to a number that can be reached by counting by twos
		A	Says the correct number and explains thinking
Ask: *"Would you check and see?"*	Says:	COUNTING BY TWOS	
		I-	Counts each cube as 2, rote counting sequence inaccurate
		I	Counts each cube as 2, rote counting sequence accurate
		P	Counts by groups of 2, rote counting sequence inaccurate
		P+	Counts by groups of 2, rote counting sequence accurate but difficult
		A	Counts by groups of 2, accurately and easily

✂ SECTION 11:

In this section, you will find the chart for summarizing what you have learned from the assessment. When you finish the assessment and excuse the children, take a moment to process what you have learned and record this information in the summary chart. The following discussion presents examples to help you see how the summary is designed and what you will want to record. Since it will be helpful later to see the date of the assessment at a glance, let the date serve as the marker in the boxes.

SUMMARIZING INSTRUCTIONAL NEEDS							
COUNTING BY FIVES				COUNTING BY TWOS			
CONSERVATION		COUNTING BY GROUPS		CONSERVATION		COUNTING BY GROUPS	
A	Says the correct number and explains thinking	A	Counts by groups with ease and accuracy	A	Says the correct number and explains thinking	A	Counts by groups with ease and accuracy
P	Ignores leftovers or restricts answer to a number that can be reached by counting by fives	P	Counts by groups, but rote sequence difficult	P	If using an odd number of cubes, restricts answer to a number that can be reached by counting by twos	P	Counts by groups, but rote sequence difficult
I	Guesses a different number	I	Moves one at a time, but counts by groups	I	Guesses a different number	I	Moves one at a time, but counts by groups

Learning to Summarize Student Information

The following example of a student interview will help you see how the summaries are designed and what type of information you might want to record.

Part One: Mrs. Kitchens places a pile of 34 cubes on the table in front of Jessy and asks her, "How many do you think are in this pile?" Jessy thinks for a moment and says, "20?" Mrs. Kitchens then asks, "How many groups of ten do you think you could make if there were 20?" "I think probably 2," Jessy says. "Go ahead and see how many groups of ten you can make," Mrs. Kitchens directs. Jessy easily organizes the cubes into piles of ten. Mrs. Kitchens notices that when she gets to 2 tens, she does not react or show any sign she is thinking about the number she estimated. When she gets done making the piles of ten, Mrs. Kitchens asks, "How many groups of ten did you make?" Jessy replies, "3." Mrs. Kitchens then asks, "How many leftovers did you have?" Jessy says, "4." Mrs. Kitchens continues, "Does that give you an idea of how many there are all together?" Jessy looks back at her piles of ten and quietly counts, "10, 20, 30...34," she says confidently. Mrs. Kitchens pushes the cubes back into a pile and asks, "How many are there now?" Jessy laughs at the question. "You didn't add anything, so it's the same," she says. "How many would there be if we added 10 more?" Mrs. Kitchens asks. Jessy begins to count using her fingers to help her keep track. "34, 35, 36, 37," she counts until she gets to 44. "There's 44," she says. Mrs. Kitchens skips the rest of the questions on page 1 of the interview and goes on to page 2.

Part Two: "How many would there be if we counted these by fives?" she asks. Jessy looks up to think, and after a minute she says, "I think there could be 50," she says. "Would you check and see?" Mrs. Kitchens asks. Jessy makes piles of 5. Then she points at each pile and counts, "5, 10, 15, 20, 25, 30." When she gets to 30, she stops for a moment and looks up at Mrs. Kitchens. "I have to count these by ones," she says questioningly. "Go ahead," says Mrs. Kitchens. Jessy counts on from 30 and reports, "There are 34." Mrs. Kitchens then asks, "How many would there be if we counted these by twos?" Jessy thinks for a minute and then says "44." Mrs. Kitchens asks her to check and see. Jessy counts by twos with more hesitation than she did when counting by fives. When she finishes, she tells Mrs. Kitchens there are 34. She makes no comment

47

and does not appear to notice that she gets the same number no matter how she counts. Mrs. Kitchens sees that Jessy is not yet aware that she can determine the total of a number by knowing the number of tens and ones. She fills out Part One of the summary in the following way.

"Grouping Tens" Summary Section from Page One:

SUMMARIZING INSTRUCTIONAL NEEDS									
GOING BACK: ONE TEN AND LEFTOVERS		**NUMBER OF TENS**		**DETERMINES QUANTITY**		**GOING ON**		**+10**	**-10**
A Knows without counting **A-** Knows, but checks		**A** Tells the number of tens	2/6	**A** Knows without counting		**A** Knows without counting			
P Figures out accurately		**I** Unable to tell the number of tens		**P** Counts by tens	2/6	**P** Figures out	2/6		
I Guesses or gets wrong answer				**I** Counts by ones		**I** Guesses or gets wrong answer			
EXTENSION:		+20		-20		7 TENS + 12			
		I	P	A	I	P	A	I	P	A

She sees that Jessy knows how to count by twos and fives but doesn't realize that the number remains the same. She fills out the summary for Part Two as follows.

"Grouping Tens" Summary Section from Page Two:

SUMMARIZING INSTRUCTIONAL NEEDS							
COUNTING BY FIVES				**COUNTING BY TWOS**			
CONSERVATION		**COUNTING BY GROUPS**		**CONSERVATION**		**COUNTING BY GROUPS**	
A Says the correct number and explains thinking		**A** Counts by groups with ease and accuracy	2/6 *not sure about leftovers*	**A** Says the correct number and explains thinking		**A** Counts by groups with ease and accuracy	A- 2/6 *some hesitation*
P Ignores leftovers or restricts answer to a number that can be reached by counting by fives		**P** Counts by groups, but rote sequence difficult		**P** If using an odd number of cubes, restricts answer to a number that can be reached by counting by twos		**P** Counts by groups, but rote sequence difficult	
I Guesses a different number	2/6	**I** Moves one at a time, but counts by groups		**I** Guesses a different number	2/6	**I** Moves one at a time, but counts by groups	

MEETING INSTRUCTIONAL NEEDS

After you have identified each student's instructional needs, it is important to find practical ways to meet these various needs. The first step is to organize the information you obtained during the individual interview so that common needs are made apparent. The Class Summary sheets for "Grouping Tens" will help you do this. Examples of the Class Summary sheets are shown below.

Transfer the individual summary information from each page of the Student Interview form onto the corresponding Class Summary sheet. This will give you an overall picture of your class, and you will be able to identify groups of children who have reached similar levels of learning and who therefore share similar instructional needs. (Blackline masters of these summary sheets can be found in the appendix. BLM 8:1 and BLM 8:2.)

C.S. THE CLASS SUMMARY SHEETS

In the upper right-hand corner of the summary sheet is a picture of connecting cubes, with some arranged into a group of ten. This identifies the set of assessment forms for Concept 8: Numbers as Tens and Ones. Look for the shaded C.S. box indicating that this is a Class Summary sheet for the "Grouping Tens" assessment. Because this particular assessment has two pages you will notice special page symbols: ⟨p. 1 ⟨p. 2

The Class Summary sheets are intentionally focused on the concept of numbers as tens and ones rather than on a series of topics. This is because you can more easily meet the range of needs in your classroom when you focus in-depth on one topic than when you try to provide individualized instruction with several topics at the same time.

Grouping Tens

Concept 8: Numbers As Tens And Ones										*Class Summary*				S.I. C.S. ⟨p.1 AW

PART ONE: ORGANIZING INTO TENS AND ONES

INDICATORS				
ONE TEN AND LEFTOVERS	**NUMBER OF TENS**	**ESTIMATE**	**DETERMINES QUANTITY**	**+10/-10**
I Guesses or gets wrong answer P Figures out accurately A- Knows, but needs to check A Knows without counting	I Unable to tell the number of tens A Tells correct number of tens	I No reaction P Reacts, no new estimate A Spontaneously makes new estimate	I Counts all by ones P Counts by tens/counts the ones A Knows without needing to count	I Guesses or gets wrong answer P Figures out A Knows without counting

NAMES	One Ten and Leftovers			Number of Tens		Determines Quantity			+10			-10			EXTENSION Comments
	I	P	A	I	A	I	P	A	I	P	A	I	P	A	

Grouping Tens (continued)

Concept 8: Numbers As Tens And Ones	Class Summary	S.I.
		C.S. p.2
		AW

PART TWO: CONSERVATION AND COUNTING BY GROUPS

INDICATORS CONSERVATION	INDICATORS COUNTING BY GROUPS
I Says a different number **P** Ignores leftovers or restricts answer to a number that can be reached by counting by fives (or twos) **A** Says the correct number and explains thinking	**I-** Counts each cube as 5 (or 2); rote counting sequence inaccurate **I** Counts each cube as 5 (or 2); rote counting sequence accurate **P** Counts by groups of 5 (or 2); rote counting sequence inaccurate **P+** Counts by groups of 5 (or 2); rote counting sequence accurate but with difficulty **A** Counts by groups of 5 (or 2); rote counting sequence accurate with ease

NAMES	COMMENTS	Conservation (By twos or fives)			Counting Objects by twos			Counting Objects by fives		
		I	P	A	I	P	A	I	P	A

Grade Level Expectations

Even with the best instruction, children do not learn the underlying structure of numbers as tens and ones at the same time or the same pace. Within every classroom there will be children working at a wide range of levels. As we learn more about how to focus instruction and maximize children's learning, we may find children able to develop understanding and competence faster than we might expect. On the other hand, children who have not had appropriate foundational experiences may not be able to do what we might expect of them under different circumstance. Therefore, the grade level expectations outlined here are intended to be a very general guideline. It is the individual achievement of each child that is important for us to know.

Because place value concepts are so complex and multi-faceted, children develop an understanding of place value concepts over a period of many years. It is not until children can think of a group of ten as one unit that we can say that they are beginning to understand place value concepts. Children in kindergarten and first grade often learn to count by tens and to recognize number patterns on a 100 chart, but that is not the same as understanding the underlying structure of numbers as tens and ones. Some children will have some understanding of this idea by the end of first grade, but most children will not understand this until the middle or end of second grade, at which time they will know 10 more and 10 less than a number without figuring it out. This is understandable when we consider that most kindergarten children and many first grade children are just transitioning from thinking of numbers as a collection of ones to seeing that numbers are composed of parts. It is in second grade that most children, if they are given appropriate experiences, will come to think of numbers as tens and ones. Some children will be in third grade before they fully understand the underlying structure of numbers to 100.

Guidelines for Providing Appropriate Experiences

Children learn more when they work at the edge of their understanding and level of competence. Children's understanding of the underlying structure of numbers as tens and ones strongly influences their ability to work with two-digit addition and subtraction and to understand place value as they work with larger and larger numbers. When children are asked to solve two and three digit problems before they understand the composition of numbers to 100, they will tend to memorize procedures they don't understand in order to do the expected work. By the same token, children who already understand the underlying structure of tens and ones need experiences that challenge their thinking and provide new opportunities for learning. The challenge is to find practical ways to deal with the range of needs evident on the Class Summary. Teaching to the edge of children's understanding can be realistically managed if you keep some basic ideas in mind.

Children can work side by side with what appears to be the same task and still be working at the level that is appropriate for each one.
It is not always necessary to provide different experiences for children with different needs. In fact, it is not only more practical, it is also more effective to provide tasks that have the potential to be experienced at a variety of levels. Three children can all be working with a task where they are to determine the number of counters   that will fit in various small jars. One child could be filling a jar with pecans and therefore ending up with less than 20 objects, another child could be working with a jar that holds up to 100 objects and another child could be comparing two different jars to determine the difference between them.

Once you have assessed your students individually, the information you have obtained will help you to efficiently interpret what you see while the children are at work, allowing you to determine quickly what they need.
It takes a long time to gather specific information about a child by observing them at work in a classroom setting, but only a few minutes through the student interview. Once you have identified the children's instructional levels in the interview, you will be able to focus on what they are doing while at work and know immediately whether they are working at an appropriate level.

You can meet children's varying needs by interacting with them while they are at work: asking questions, providing support, and posing challenges when appropriate.

The following is an example of how a teacher who knows the individual needs of her students interacts with them during math time.

This group of second-grade children has been working with a set of eight place value stations for several days. All of the stations require children to organize cubes into tens and ones. Mr. Torres knows the children are familiar with all the activities that are out at the stations. When the whole group gathers after station time is over, the children discuss various ways they found they could keep track of the tens and ones. Everyone has had an opportunity to consider how to organize their materials in ways that help them determine the numbers of tens and ones. Today Mr. Torres is watching the group who have chosen to work with the activity called Lots of Lines so he can see where they are in their developing understanding. The children are measuring the lines on the Lots of Lines task cards with colored paper clips. Mr. Torres sees at a glance that three of the children have marked the tens and one child has not. Pia and Levi have organized by using ten of one color followed by ten of another color. Jon has used blue paper clips but has marked each ten with one green paper clip. Yolanda has used lots of different colors and has not organized them in any apparent way. Mr. Torres decides to ask the children to tell him how many they have so far. This will give him the information he needs to find out who can use the organization of the tens and ones in determining the total and who cannot. He sees that Pia has lined up 10 green paper clips, 10 yellow paper clips and so far has 6 white paper clips. Pia responds to his question by saying, "I have 2 tens and 6, so far. So that is 26." When Mr. Torres assessed Pia, she was still counting by tens, so he is pleased to see she is beginning to see the relationship between the number of tens and the total. When Levi is asked how many he has so far, he counts the three groups of tens and the four extras. "Ten, twenty, thirty, thirty-one, thirty-two, thirty-three, thirty-four," he counts. "I have thirty-four," he reports. When Yolanda is asked how many she has so far, she recounts them all by ones. Mr. Torres is aware that Yolanda is not using tens and ones as yet, but since she needs to work with simply counting large groups, he feels she is getting the practice she needs.

Ask questions that will help children think about the concept you want them to learn.

For example:

"Is there a way for you to organize your counters so it is easy for you to keep track of what you have?"
"How many tens do you think you can make?"
"Now that you have this many tens, do you have another idea of what it could be?"
"I see you have organized your tiles into tens and ones. How many do you have so far?"
"Now that you know how many tens and leftovers there are, does that help you know how many altogether?"
"What did you notice?"

Meet with small groups when particular needs can best be met through teacher-directed activities.

Although many of the children's instructional needs can be met by providing activities that meet a range of needs, some instructional needs are best met through small group work. Children who need prerequisite experiences or help focusing on the underlying ideas you are working with will benefit greatly from small group teacher-directed activities. On the other hand, children who need practice to develop proficiency and accuracy need more time with independent practice, accompanied by interactions with the teacher about their work.

The following is an example of how a teacher who knows his students' individual needs supports children's learning during a small group activity.

Mr. Torres calls Yolanda and three other children to work with him in a small group. When he assessed this group of children, he found that they were not yet making the connection between two-digit numbers and groups of ten. He is having them work with ten-frames, as this is a concrete way for children to count tens. He passes out a ten frame to each child. They are going to take turns rolling a 1-6 die. The object is to see how many ten frames they can fill. Yolanda rolls first and gets a 5. She places 5 cubes on her board and hands the die to Casey. Casey rolls the die and gets a 3, puts 3 cubes on his ten-frame, and hands the die to the next child. After each child has had a turn, it starts around the circle again. This time the group tells how many needed on each ten-frame to complete the ten. It's Yolanda's turn. "How many does she need to fill up her frame?" Mr. Torres asks. The children are to signal when they have figured the answer out by raising their thumb. Mr. Torres calls on Casey, who says that Yolanda needs 5 more. Mr. Torres is pleased that Casey knew that immediately, as that is a new skill for him. When Yolanda rolls a 6, the children are excited. They know she has enough to make a ten and to start a new ten-frame. The game continues for a few more minutes. Each time another ten frame is filled, he asks, "How many tens do we have now?" He wants the children to realize they can count tens as single entities. Using the ten frames is one way for them to experience this idea. When the game ends, they have filled 5 ten-frames. Each time they got one more ten frame, he wrote the number of tens and the total number of cubes . When they had filled 2 ten-frames, Jackie wanted to share something he had figured out. "What did you figure out, Jackie?" Mr. Torres asks. "I already know how many in two of these. It's 20. 10 and 10 is 20," Jackie says excitedly.

Mr. Torres is pleased that Jackie has a way to determine the answer without counting. He notices as the game proceeds, however, that Jackie cannot use that information to help tell how many for any other number. Now, he challenges the children to figure out how many in all 5 frames. They can actually count the cubes or use empty ten frames if they need them. When they think they know how many, they are to write it down and give their papers to Mr. Torres, and then go back to work at the independent stations. Mr. Torres will continue exploring the idea of counting tens with this group of children.

ASSESSING CHILDREN AT WORK

Observing children's progress as they work is an important part of the daily life of the classroom. Once you have assessed your children through the student interview and have determined their instructional needs, much information about the children's growth in understanding and competence can be gained by observing them over time while they are at work. Sometimes, however, it may be useful to do a more systematic check of their progress and record specific data related to a particular concept for each of the children. The assessment tasks and recording sheets included here are designed to give you a focused way to keep track of children's ongoing progress understanding numbers as tens and ones.

It is recommended that one area be set up as the assessment station where a few children at a time can work with the assessment task while the rest of the children work at other independent station tasks. Over a period of a few days, you will be able to observe all the children you intend to assess.

Record the information that you obtain during the observation on the Assessing at Work forms. This can then be used along with the Class Summary sheets, or you can transfer the information to the Class Summary sheets to show the progress the children have made.

A.W. ASSESSING CHILDREN AT WORK: MEASURING SHAPES

An example of the Assessing Children at Work form for "Measuring Shapes" is on the following page. In the upper right-hand corner of each are pictures of connecting cubes, with some organized into a group of ten. This identifies the set of assessment forms for Concept 8: Numbers as Tens and Ones. The box on each form labeled A.W. is shaded, indicating that this is the Assessing at Work form. The form includes questions to guide your observations and indicators that help you interpret what you see. The indicators are the same as those used for the student interview, "Grouping Tens."

Getting to Know the Assessment Task: "Measuring Shapes"

The task "Measuring Shapes" requires children to measure the area of various paper shapes with tiles or cubes. They organize the tiles or cubes into tens and ones and use that information to determine the total.

"Measuring Shapes"

Concept 8: Numbers As Tens And Ones

Assessing at Work

| S.I. |
| CS. |
| A.W. |

YOU NEED:
Paper Shapes (BLM 8:4-13)
Tiles or Cubes (50-100 per student)
Paper and Pencil

GOAL:
To determine if the child can use tens and ones to determine how many.

PROCEDURE:
The children record their estimate of the number of tens and ones it will take to cover a Paper Shape. They cover the shape, organizing the tiles or cubes into tens and ones, and record the total. Ask, "How many will there be if we add 10? ...How many if we take 10 away?"

WHAT ARE WE LOOKING FOR?	INDICATORS	
Estimation Are they willing to estimate? Are they comfortable (and honest) with their estimates, or do they try to change them to match their answers? Can they use the information they get as they work, and change their minds as they go? Do they get closer to the actual amount?	**I** **P** **A**	Unwilling to estimate or changes estimate to match answer, or can't adjust to get closer Adjusts the estimate when the task is nearly completed Adjusts estimate and gets closer midway through the task
Determines the Quantity Using Tens and Ones Do they organize their work into tens and ones? What methods do they use? When they determine an amount, do they count them all by ones? Do they count by tens? Do they know quantities as soon as the tens and ones are known?	**I** **P** **A**	Counts all by ones Counts the tens and then the ones accurately Instantly knows total when number of tens and ones is known
Plus 10/Minus 10 Do they know, without counting, how many there will be when adding ten more? Taking ten away?	**I** **P** **A**	Guesses or gets wrong answer Figures out Knows without counting
Writing Two-Digit Numbers Are they able to record the quantities appropriately?	**I** **P** **A**	Incorrect Takes effort, makes some errors Writes correctly with ease

NAMES	ESTIMATES			DETERMINES QUANTITY			+10			-10			COMMENTS (Includes Writing Two-Digit Numbers)
	I	P	A	I	P	A	I	P	A	I	P	A	

Checking for Ongoing Progress

As you observe the children at work, check to see how they determine the total area of the Paper Shape. How are they keeping track of their tens? Are they able to determine the total once they know the number of tens and ones, or do they need to count? Interrupt them while they are working and see if they can they tell you how many they have thus far. Also ask them if they want to change their estimate now that they have more information about the Paper Shape they are working with. Once they have completed the task, ask them "How many would there be if we added 10 more? What if we took 10 away?"

Guidelines for Observing Children

♦**Make sure children are already familiar with the task.**
It is more efficient if the children are familiar with the task so you are not taking time to teach them how to do the task during this assessment time, but rather are using the task as a tool for determining the stage of their learning.

♦**Be clear about what you are watching for.**
You can learn many things about a child while watching them at work, but to make this kind of assessment manageable, you need to focus specifically on what you need to know to make instructional decisions or report progress. To guide your observations, refer to the questions included with the assessment form.

♦**Focus on just one child at a time.**
Don't try to watch too many children at once. Once you have made sure that all the children know what to do and are busy working at the task, you will be more efficient if you focus on one child at a time until you have the information you need.

♦**Just gather the information. Don't stop and teach.**
The point of the assessment task is to check and record what the children know so far and is not a teaching time. If you just observe and record what the children are able to do, you will be able to watch several children within a short period of time.

LINKING ASSESSMENT AND INSTRUCTION

After you have identified the needs of the children, you will be better able to provide appropriate experiences using whatever instructional materials you have available. The following charts explain the instructional needs of students for each of the indicators on the assessment and refer you to particular activities from the *Developing Number Concepts* series to aid those who have access to these resources. The *Developing Number Concepts* series includes both teacher-directed and independent activities specifically designed to meet the varying needs of students.

There are three books in the series:

    Book 1: Developing Number Concepts: Counting, Comparing and Pattern
    Book 2: Developing Number Concepts: Addition and Subtraction
    Book 3: Developing Number Concepts: Place Value, Multiplication and Division

The activities in each book are coded for easy access. For example, "1:2-23" refers to Book 1, Chapter 2, Activity Number 23.

Providing Appropriate Experiences for Understanding Numbers as Tens and Ones

When you are helping children develop proficiency understanding numbers as tens and ones, it is important to recognize that competency develops over time. Present a variety of activities, allowing children to experience organizing numbers into tens and ones in many different situations over several days or even weeks. This will help them make generalizations and integrate their ideas about the underlying structure of numbers. Let their responses dictate the amount of time you spend before moving on.

One Ten and Leftovers: Going Back

If you have children who needed to be assessed with the Going Back section of the assessment, which focuses on identifying the number of ones in teen numbers, provide the following experiences:

Those children who guessed or got the wrong answer "need instruction" (I) and should be given teacher-directed experiences asking them to combine one ten with various leftovers. This will help them focus on the pattern that emerges when ten is added to a single digit number.

Children who can figure out the number of leftovers in a teen number "need practice" (P) until they know this without figuring it out. Give them experiences where they are asked to focus on organizing numbers into one ten and leftovers. Pay particular attention to how they determine the totals.

Those children who know the number of tens and ones in numbers from 10 to 19 are "ready to apply" (A) and should move on to work with the structure of numbers as tens and ones as described in the following section.

If children "need instruction" (I) combining numbers that are organized into one ten and leftovers:
Provide experiences working with numbers that are arranged into a group of one ten and some more, such as those listed below from Developing Number Concepts, Book 2.

NEEDS INSTRUCTION (I)			
TEACHER DIRECTED **Combining and Separating One Ten and Some More**			
2:3-30	Working with Ten-Shapes	Addition: Ten Plus a Number	Subtraction: Minus Ten
2:3-31	A Ten-Shape and More: Subtraction (Do the readiness activity described within this activity.)		

If children "need practice" (P) combining one ten and some ones:
Provide experiences working with numbers that require them to organize numbers into a group of one ten and leftovers and determine the total, such as those listed below from Developing Number Concepts, Book 2.

NEEDS PRACTICE (P)					
TEACHER DIRECTED **Combining and Separating One Ten and Some More**					
2:3-30	Working with Ten-Shapes	Addition: Nine Plus a Number	Addition: Eight Plus a Number	Addition: Mixing Them Up	Subtraction: Minus Nine
2:3-31	A Ten-Shape and More: Subtraction				
INDEPENDENT ACTIVITIES **Combining and Separating One Ten and Some More**					
2:3-34	Two Ten-Shapes: Addition Station				
2:3-35	A Ten-Shape and More: Subtraction Station				

Numbers as Tens and Ones

If children "need instruction" with either identifying the number of tens in a number (I) or determining the quantity by using tens and ones (I), give them experiences forming and counting groups of four, five and six before working with groups of ten. Children must realize that they can count groups as though they were single entities before they can fully understand that numbers are composed of groups of tens and ones. Working with groups consisting of various amounts helps them make that generalization.

If children "need practice" (P), give them experiences organizing cubes into groups of tens and ones until they can tell the total number without needing to count by tens to do so. When children need to count by tens to determine how many, they do not yet see the relationship between the particular number of tens and ones and the total number of objects. They need a variety of experiences organizing tens and ones in many different ways in order to develop meaning for this complex idea.

If children are "ready to apply" (A) the concept of numbers as tens and ones, give them experiences comparing groups of tens and ones. This will help make these numbers meaningful for them and will help them learn the particular relationships between quantities. These relationships will also be important when solving comparative subtraction problems.

If children "need instruction" (I) identifying the number of tens in a number or determining the total of a number:
Provide experiences where children form and count groups, such as those listed below from Developing Number Concepts, Book 3.

NEEDS INSTRUCTION (I)	
TEACHER DIRECTED **Forming and Counting Groups**	
3: p. 15-38	The Grouping Games
INDEPENDENT ACTIVITIES **Forming and Counting Groups**	
3:1-17	Recording Various Number Patterns
3:1-18	Grab and Add

If children "need practice" (P) determining quantities by using tens and ones:
Provide experiences with the Grouping Games listed in the chart on page 36. Also provide activities that give children opportunities to organize cubes into groups of ten, such as those listed below from Developing Number Concepts, Book 3.

NEEDS PRACTICE (P)	
INDEPENDENT ACTIVITIES **Forming and Counting Groups**	
3:1-32	Lots of Lines, Level 1
3:1-33	Paper Shapes, Level 1
3:1-34	Yarn, Level 1
3:1-35	Yarn Shapes, Level 1
3:1-36	Containers, Level 1
3:1-37	Cover It Up, Level 1
3:1-38	Measuring Things in the Room, Level 1
3:1-39	Measuring Myself, Level 1
3:1-40	Comparing Myself
3:1-41	Making Trails
3:1-42	Building Stacks
3:1-43	Race to 100
3:1-44	Race to Zero

If children "ready to apply" (A) the concept of numbers as tens and ones:
Provide experiences comparing quantities such as those described below from Developing Number Concepts, Book 3.

READY TO APPLY (A)	
INDEPENDENT ACTIVITIES Forming and Counting Groups	
3:1-32	Lots of Lines, Levels 2 and 3
3:1-33	Paper Shapes, Levels 2 and 3
3:1-34	Yarn, Levels 2 and 3
3:1-35	Yarn Shapes, Extension
3:1-36	Containers, Levels 2 and 3
3:1-37	Cover It Up, Levels 2 and 3
3:1-38	Measuring Things in the Room, Levels 2 and 3
3:1-39	Measuring Myself, Levels 2 and 3
3:1-40	Comparing Myself

Adding Ten or Taking Away Ten

If children "need instruction (I) or practice (P)" adding ten or taking ten away, continue to have them work with the activities presented earlier that are designed to help them understand the composition of number to 100. When children understand the underlying structure of tens, they will be able to add one more ten or take one ten away without counting.

If children "ready to apply" (A) adding or taking away ten, give them opportunities to compare numbers as listed above as well as work adding and subtracting two-digit numbers. More information about two-digit addition and subtraction can be found in *Assessing Math Concepts: Assessment 9: Two-Digit Addition and Subtraction.*

Estimation

Many of the activities listed in the charts above ask the children to estimate before determining the actual quantity. This is to focus their attention on number relationships and help them develop a sense of the quantity of the numbers they are working with. Estimating causes children to pay attention to the quantities and to reflect on whether it is what they expected it to be or not.

Whenever children are determining how many, ask questions such as:
"Before you count, can you guess how many you think it will be?"
"Now that you have counted some of them, do you have a different idea?"

Notice: Are the children making sensible estimates?
Do they notice if their estimates are close or not?
Do they change their minds about the total after counting some of the objects?
Do their new estimates get closer?

APPENDIX

BLACKLINE MASTERS

BLM 8:1   CLASS SUMMARY SHEET (PAGE 1)

BLM 8:2   CLASS SUMMARY SHEET (PAGE 2)

BLM 8:3   ASSESSING AT WORK FORM

BLM 8:4-13   PAPER SHAPES

Grouping Tens

S.I.

C.S. p.1

AW

PART ONE: ORGANIZING INTO TENS AND ONES

INDICATORS

ONE TEN AND LEFTOVERS	NUMBER OF TENS	ESTIMATE	DETERMINES QUANTITY	+10/-10
I Guesses or gets wrong answer P Figures out accurately A- Knows, but needs to check A Knows without counting	I Unable to tell the number of tens A Tells correct number of tens	I No reaction P Reacts, no new estimate A Spontaneously makes new estimate	I Counts all by ones P Counts by tens/ counts the ones A Knows without needing to count	I Guesses or gets wrong answer P Figures out A Knows without counting

NAMES	One Ten and Leftovers			Number of Tens		Determines Quantity			+10			-10			EXTENSION Comments
	I	P	A	I	A	I	P	A	I	P	A	I	P	A	

S.I.

C.S. ▸ p.2

AW

PART TWO: CONSERVATION AND COUNTING BY GROUPS

INDICATORS CONSERVATION	INDICATORS COUNTING BY GROUPS
I Says a different number **P** Ignores leftovers or restricts answer to a number that can be reached by counting by fives (or twos) **A** Says the correct number and explains thinking	**I-** Counts each cube as 5 (or 2); rote counting sequence inaccurate **I** Counts each cube as 5 (or 2); rote counting sequence accurate **P** Counts by groups of 5 (or 2); rote counting sequence inaccurate **P+** Counts by groups of 5 (or 2); rote counting sequence accurate but with difficulty **A** Counts by groups of 5 (or 2); rote counting sequence accurate with ease

NAMES	COMMENTS	Conservation (By twos or fives)			Counting Objects by twos			Counting Objects by fives		
		I	P	A	I	P	A	I	P	A

"Measuring Shapes"

Concept 8: Numbers As Tens And Ones

Assessing at Work

S.I.

C.S.

A.W.

YOU NEED:
Paper Shapes (BLM 8:4-13)
Tiles or Cubes (50-100 per student)
Paper and Pencil

GOAL:
To determine if the child can use tens and ones to determine how many.

PROCEDURE:
The children record their estimate of the number of tens and ones it will take to cover a Paper Shape. They cover the shape, organizing the tiles or cubes into tens and ones, and record the total. Ask, "How many will there be if we add 10? ...How many if we take 10 away?"

WHAT ARE WE LOOKING FOR?	INDICATORS
Estimation Are they willing to estimate? Are they comfortable (and honest) with their estimates, or do they try to change them to match their answers? Can they use the information they get as they work, and change their minds as they go? Do they get closer to the actual amount?	**I** Unwilling to estimate or changes estimate to match answer, or can't adjust to get closer **P** Adjusts the estimate when the task is nearly completed **A** Adjusts estimate and gets closer midway through the task
Determines the Quantity Using Tens and Ones Do they organize their work into tens and ones? What methods do they use? When they determine an amount, do they count them all by ones? Do they count by tens? Do they know quantities as soon as the tens and ones are known?	**I** Counts all by ones **P** Counts the tens and then the ones accurately **A** Instantly knows total when number of tens and ones is known
Plus 10/Minus 10 Do they know, without counting, how many there will be when adding ten more? Taking ten away?	**I** Guesses or gets wrong answer **P** Figures out **A** Knows without counting
Writing Two-Digit Numbers Are they able to record the quantities appropriately?	**I** Incorrect **P** Takes effort, makes some errors **A** Writes correctly with ease

NAMES	ESTIMATES			DETERMINES QUANTITY			+10			-10			COMMENTS (Includes Writing Two-Digit Numbers)
	I	P	A	I	P	A	I	P	A	I	P	A	

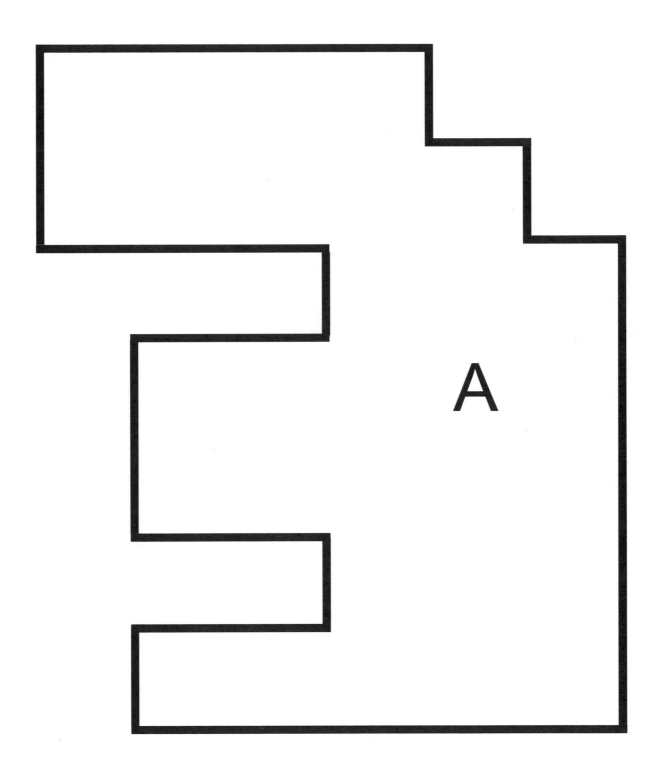

A

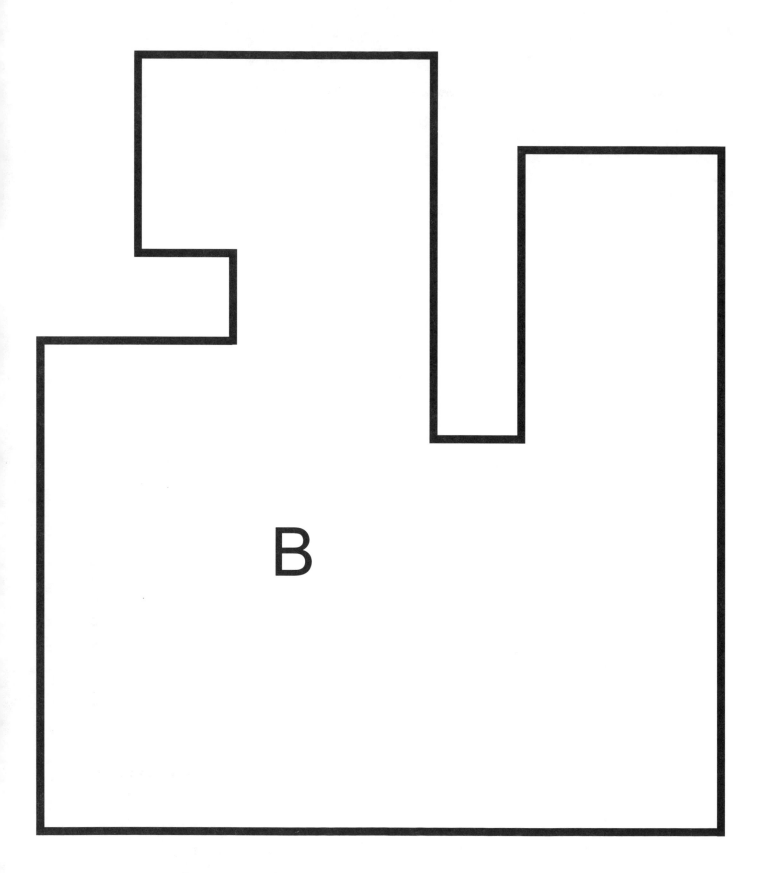

B

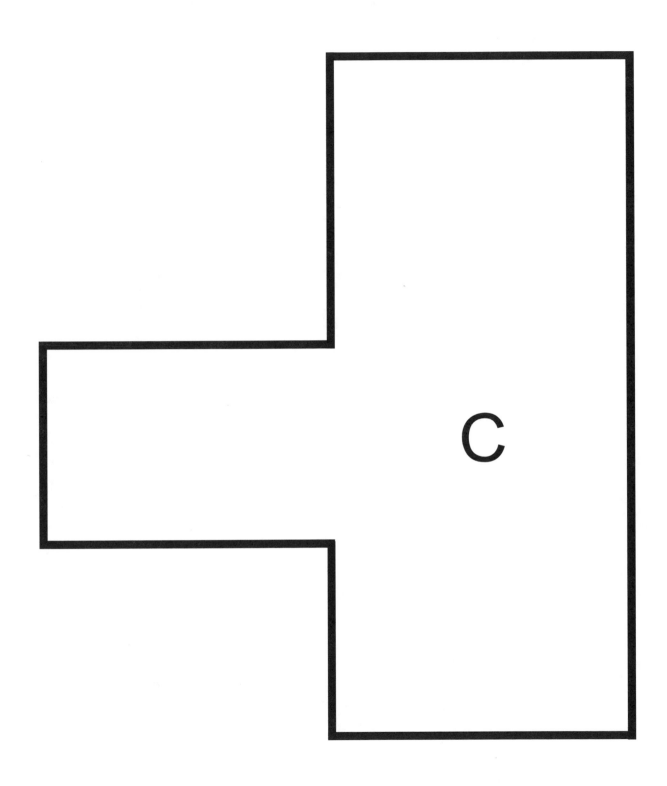

C

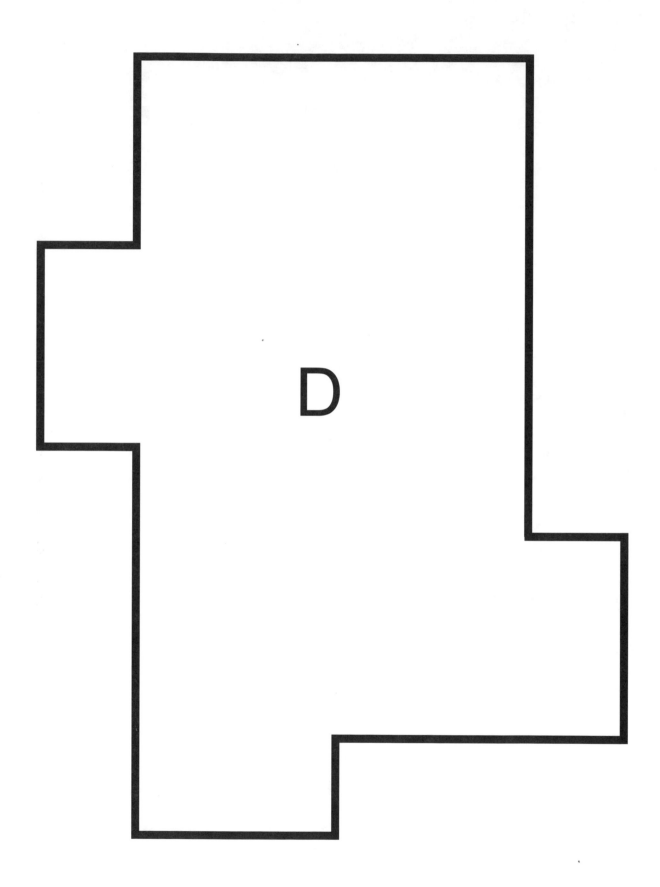

D

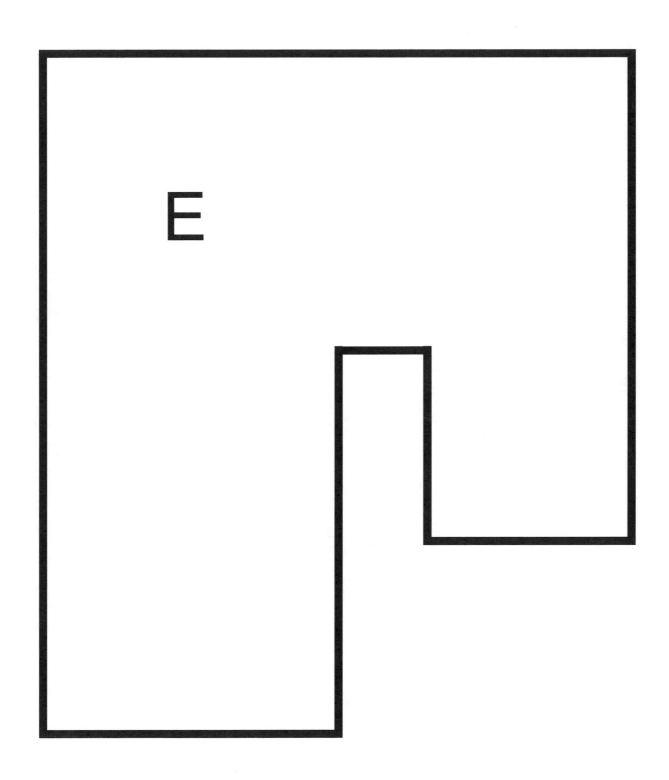

E

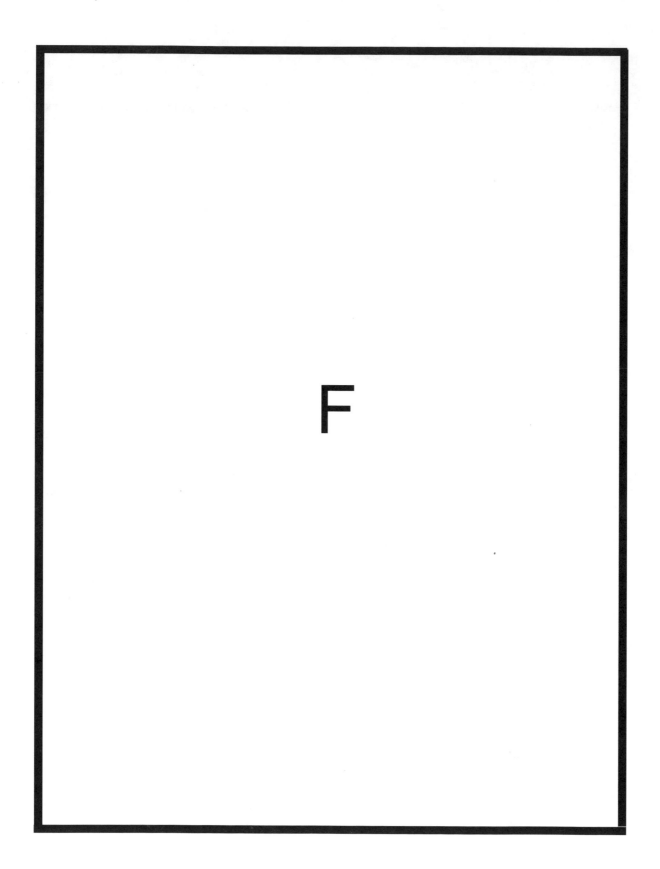

F

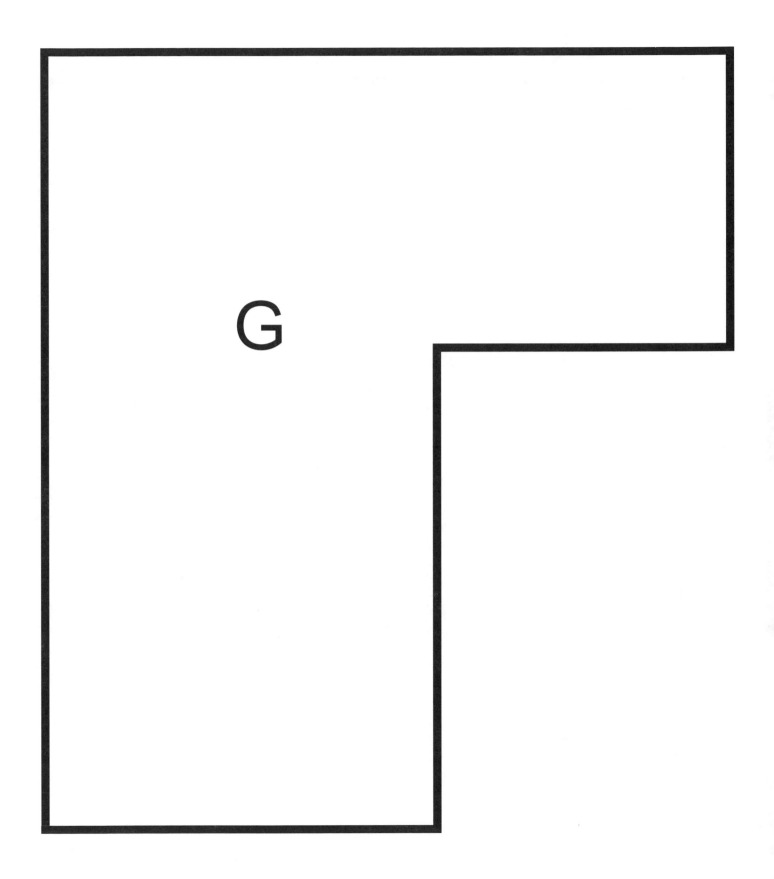

G

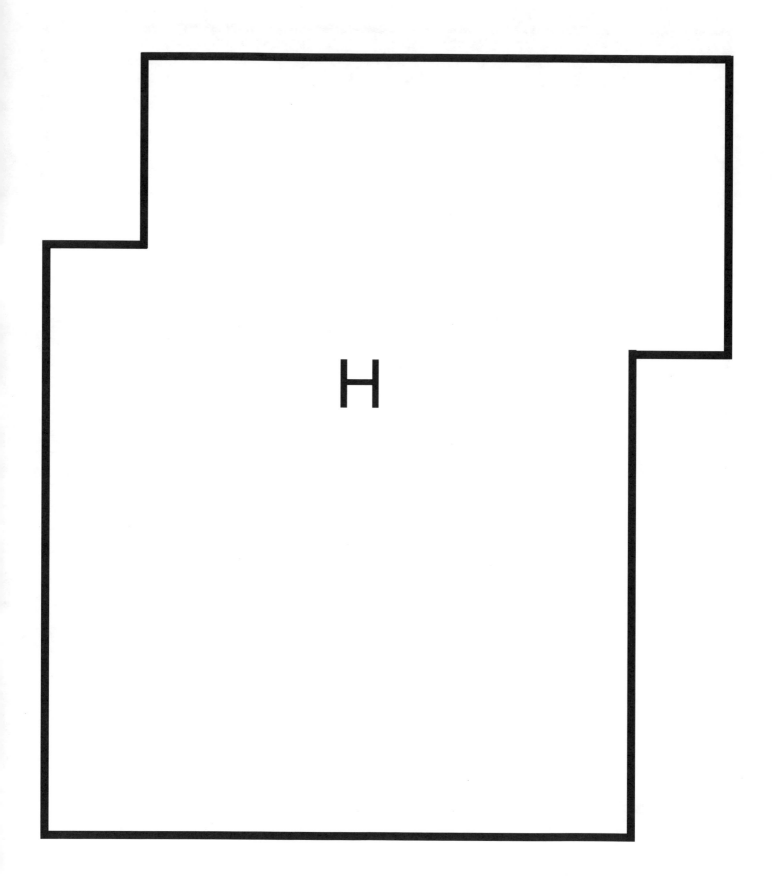

H

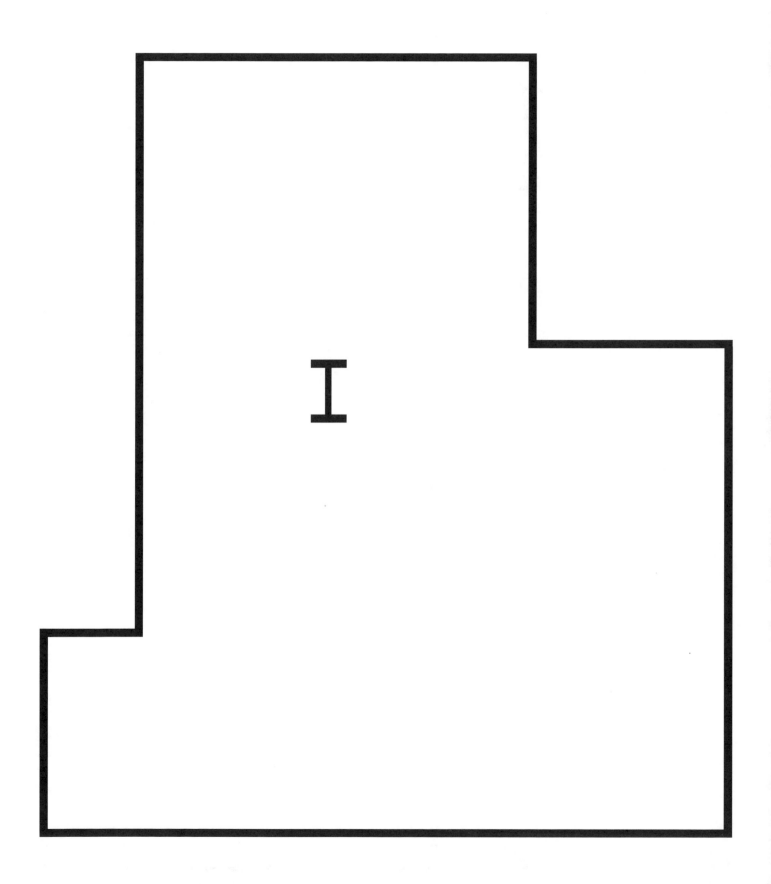

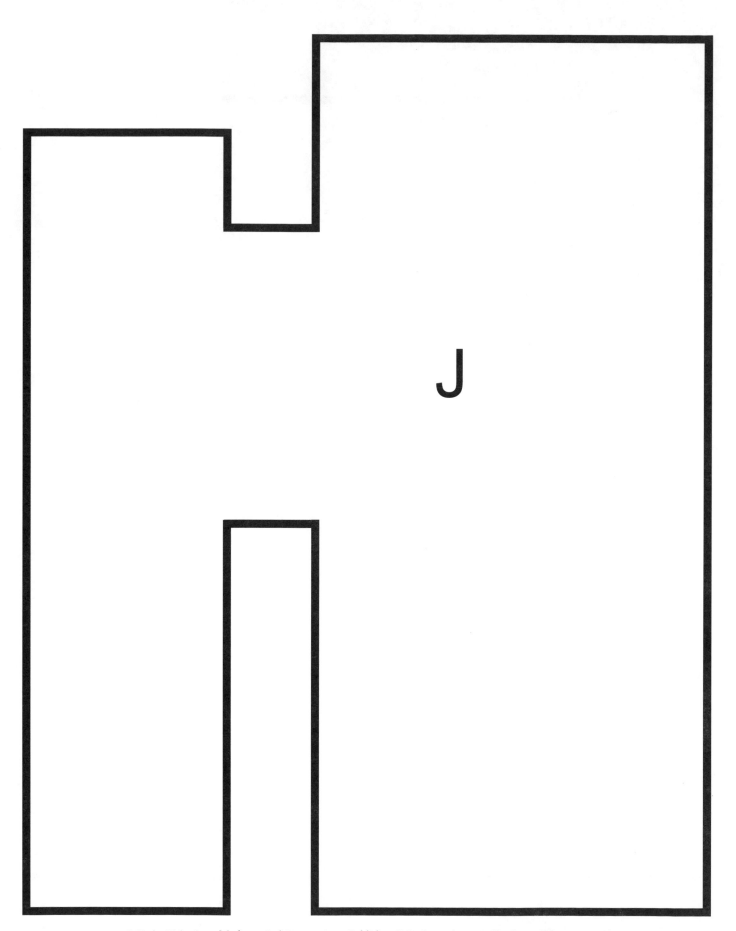

J